ELITE STEAM

Michael Harris

To all British steam enginemen

Atlantic Transport Publishers
Trevithick House, West End, Penryn,
Cornwall TR10 8HE

ISBN: 0 906899 71 0

First published 1996

© Michael Harris 1996

This book is based on a series of articles first published
in *Steam World*

Design and layout: Trevor Ridley
Printed in Great Britain by Lavenham Press

British Cataloguing in Publication Data
A catalogue record for this book is available from
the British Library

CONTENTS

INTRODUCTION   4

ACKNOWLEDGEMENTS   5

Chapter 1   'USING THE ENGINE AS BEST WE COULD'   8

Chapter 2   THROWING DOWN THE GAUNTLET   18

Chapter 3   A TALE OF BURNISHED BUFFERS   29

Chapter 4   RESPECTED BUT NOT LOVED   41

Chapter 5   NINE ELMS AND THE PACKETS   54

Chapter 6   'THE TALK OF THE LINE'   68

Chapter 7   LIVING WITH THE ARISTOCRACY   83

Chapter 8   'FEET UP, DON, IT'S TRING'   93

Chapter 9   'WHEN I START, DIG IN!'   107

Chapter 10   'IN A HOTTER PLACE YE COULDNA BE'   123

Chapter 11   RULE BRITANNIA   136

INTRODUCTION

I suppose that if, like me, you had spent your impressionable years under the spell of the steam locomotive, then that fascination will never pall. It was a second-hand experience in the sense that the inhabitants of the platform-ends at Paddington, Euston, King's Cross, Waterloo - or wherever - participated in a spectator sport. Enginemen were generally friendly, perhaps tolerant is a better word, when it came to their spectators. Some were prepared to exchange a few words because many enginemen needed little encouragement to talk about their engines. It was less likely though that you would have a chance to talk at length to a driver or fireman away from the hiss of escaping steam.

I was able to meet a driver at a relatively early age and, to some extent, my memories of the late Jim Dow serve as an inspiration for this book which incorporates material that appeared first as articles in *Steam World* magazine. My thanks, and those of my publisher, are due to Emap Apex magazines and, more directly, to my good friend Chris Leigh, Editor of *Steam World,* for their willingness that the articles should appear collectively. In the process, they have been expanded, the result of much valuable information that came to me from readers in response to the articles.

I have added an introductory chapter, by way of explanation for much that appears in the succeeding chapters. Also, Chapter 11 features a depot that did not form the subject of a *Steam World* article. I had wanted to make reference to BR Standard engines, and a keenness to applaud the largely unsung work of Clacton shed provided a perfect opportunity to combine the two.

In preparing the articles, my intention was that each would highlight a particular theme, irrespective of the depot being featured. Hence, Chapter 2 'Throwing down the gauntlet' looks at a depot which took pride in making the most of relatively modest engines on Top Link duties, and in so doing its crews established a notable record for excellent and consistent performances. Chapter 3 'A Tale of Burnished Buffers' considers the realities of lodging or double-home turns in earlier postwar years against the background of poor coal and indifferent morale, and how that situation was transformed. Chapter 4 'Respected, but not loved' looks at the use of Pacific locomotives on high-mileage turns. Chapter 5

'Nine Elms and the Packets' reviews enginemen's attitudes towards the Bulleid Pacifics, and the case for rebuilding them. Chapter 6 'The Talk of the Line' provides an opportunity to review the working of cross-country expresses in the steam age, and the requirements for reliability. Chapter 7 'Living with the Aristocracy' concentrates on the railway community surrounding a locomotive depot. Chapter 8 'Feet up, Don, it's Tring' attempts to appreciate why young men were drawn to footplate work - and what that involved. Chapter 9 'When I start, dig in!' focusses on a depot whose crews experienced a wide range of express passenger work, and numerous special workings. Chapter 10 'In a hotter place ye couldna be' looks at the community of railwaymen at one of the largest depots. Chapter 11 'Rule Britannia' is a reminder that express passenger turns were not necessarily the preserve of depots with household names.

In every case, I am extremely grateful for the many enginemen who agreed to talk to me, and also for the encouragement of railway friends who felt that an account of everyday work should appear in print. They kindly provided me with introductions to former enginemen who had so much to tell me of their experiences. I feel that I have been privileged to meet some of the nicest people I have had the fortune to encounter. Several invited me into their homes, and all took considerable trouble with my questions, and I am indebted to them. I trust that in the Acknowledgements I have fairly given due credit for their help, and to many others, too.

As with so many enginemen, Jim Dow was a memorable raconteur. He had stepped down from the footplate some years previously, but his memories of the job had not dimmed. I can see him now, tall and with a quizzical smile, as he described the travails of Corkerhill men with those Stanier's '5Xs' ('Jubilees') that retained the original type of boiler with a low degree of superheating. He had no difficulty remembering the numbers of those involved. 'Och, they were ter-r-rible! Fifty-six forty-three; fifty-six forty-four; fifty-six forty-five; fifty-six forty-six...Och, dear...They wouldna steam the length of your arm!'

Michael Harris
Ottershaw, Surrey 1996

ACKNOWLEDGEMENTS

In the preparation of Chapters 2-11, and as an acknowledgment of their time, their reminiscences and their information, I should like to record my appreciation and grateful thanks to the following:

Chapter 2 Throwing down the gauntlet

R. Brazier (ex-Driver, Bushbury) and Mrs Brazier; George W.F. Green (engine diagramming Derby and Crewe); J. Hurley (former Passed Cleaner, Bushbury), and Ken Phillips.

Chapter 3 A tale of burnished buffers

Bruce Joyce and Alan Vickery (both former cleaners, firemen and drivers at Landore, later Western Region traction inspectors) and Mrs Joyce, and also Ted Abear (former fireman and driver, Old Oak Common), Philip Atkins, Dennis Flood, A. J. Owen, Bill Peto, Ken Phillips, and David Tomkiss.

Chapter 4 Respected, but not loved

Andy Robson (former fireman and driver Gateshead and Newcastle), Philip Atkins, Ian S. Carr, Harry Friend (fireman, driver and traction inspector, Gateshead), and Ken Phillips.

Chapter 5 Nine Elms and the Packets

Phil Bassett, John Churchill and Eric Youldon. I wish to acknowledge reference made to published articles by Bert Hooker, Peter Winding, and the late Fred Prickett. I am indebted to Keith Moore, Senior Librarian and Archivist of the Institution of Mechanical Engineers who permitted me to examine not only the drivers' testimonial held in the Library, but also the correspondence between Alan Wilton and O. V. S. Bulleid.

Chapter 6 'The Talk of the Line'

Len and Trevor Glasspool, Tom King and Dennis Moriarty

(all enginemen from Bristol Barrow Rd), and the assistance of Mrs Glasspool, Tom Clift and Colin Forse. George W. Green has kindly made available details of LMR engine diagrams and men's rosters. Others who have provided invaluable material include: C. R. Abson (ex-fireman, Bournville), John Childs, Don Flook and Bob Dearnning (fitters, Barrow Road), C. W. Portch and M. H. Quirk (cleaner and fireman at Barrow Rd).

Chapter 7 Living with the aristocracy

Ron Dansie whom I first met all those years ago at the regulator of 'B1' No 61298, and Mrs Dansie. The Community History Library & Archive of the London Borough of Brent and, in particular, to Adam Spencer and Bridget Keane.

Chapter 8 'Feet up, Don, it's Tring'

Don Buckley and Alan Corfield, and also Dennis Flood for making it all possible.

Chapter 9 'When I start, dig in!'

Ted Abear for his time, his reminiscences, his photographs and, above all, his interest.

Chapter 10 'In a hotter place ye couldna be'

Ian Lamb, William McLagan and Robert Taylor. I would not have met them were it not for the kind introductions made by Allan Baker. Bernard Boyce provided hospitality at Polmadie itself. To the Scottish Record Office for research facilities which included access to the McLagan Collection and permission to reproduce material included in Chapter 1. Reference is made to *Steam Lines*, edited by W. McLagan and published by Famedram Publishers Ltd in 1973.

Chapter 11 Rule Britannia

Fred Barral, Cliff Cockaday, Dick Hardy, Colin Swettenham and Dennis Webb. I would not have met Fred, Cliff and Colin had it not been for the kind introduction made by Dick

Hardy, and Colin and his wife so kindly provided hospitality in their home at Clacton which helped stimulate an enjoyable conversation.

In Chapter 1, I have acknowledged the source of observations and information thus: Alan Corfield (Edge Hill), the commentator's main depot being shown in brackets. I have also included quotes from enginemen met in course of other work, and with whom I have corresponded. This is an opportunity to record my thanks to them. The 30 or so diaries written up by George Merry are available for inspection at the National Railway Museum Reading Room, by written application to the Librarian, Philip Atkins.

This book has also relied heavily on the kindness and goodwill of various photographers. In particular thanks are due to Brian Stephenson for photo research, and the provision of prints to an exemplary standard from the Rail Archive Stephenson for most of the chapters, and for the colour transparencies from the K. L. Cook Collection used on the dust-jacket. He also most kindly produced prints from the negatives of other photographers. Gavin Morrison most helpfully located a suitable shed scene from his transparency collection to feature on the dust-jacket.

To many, memories of the Barrow Road 'Jubilees', and 'Castles' at work in the Bristol area and in South Wales are associated with the wonderfully atmospheric photographs of George Heiron who has specially provided prints for reproduction in two of the chapters, for which I am most grateful.

I would also like to thank Ian S. Carr, Lewis Coles, Brian Morrison and Dick Riley for providing me with copies of their photographs, and Graham Stacey for supplying me with prints from the Photomatic Collection. Chris Bishop has most kindly read the proofs and made useful suggestions.

In all my work with the articles and in the preparation of the book, my long-suffering family have been so patient and shown such interest, that I would like to record my thanks to you, Carol, Edmund and Georgia, and the ever-companionable Susie.

I should be delighted to hear from anyone wishing to make comments on the book, or with material to contribute. Would you be so kind as to write to me c/o the Publisher – Atlantic Books, Trevithick House, West End, Penryn, Cornwall TR10 8HE Thank you!

Bibliography

Philip S. Bagwell, *The Railwaymen*, Vol 1 (George Allen & Unwin, 1963)

Paul Bolger, *BR Motive Power Depots* – one for each Region (Ian Allan, 1984)

Driver L. A. Earl, *Speeding North with the 'Royal Scot'* (Oxford University Press, 1939)

R. H. N. Hardy, *Steam in the Blood* (Ian Allan, 1971)

T. R. Gourvish, *British Railways 1948-73* (Cambridge University Press, 1986)

J. T. Hodgson and J. Williams, *Locomotive management from cleaning to driving* ('The Railway Engineer, 1908 et seq)

Locomotives of the LNER Parts 2A, 2B, 3C (Railway Correspondence & Travel Society, various dates)

Norman McKillop, *The Lighted Flame* (Nelson, 1950)

O. S. Nock, *British Railways in Action* (Nelson, 1956)

P. Ransome-Wallis, *Men of the Footplate* (Ian Allan, 1954)

J. R. Raynes, *Engines and Men* (Goodall & Suddick, 1921)

Driver J. W. Street, *I Drove the 'Cheltenham Flyer'* (Nicholson & Watson, 1951)

P. N. Townend, *Top Shed* (Ian Allan, 2nd Edition, 1989)

Various documents in the Public Record Office, in particular the Southern Area Board Minutes (eg AN 103/26); Western Area Board Minutes (eg AN 103/26, AN 119/3, AN 119/4, AN 119/5), minutes of meetings of superintendents (AN 119/9); Railway Executive report for 1951 (AN 88/54).

Engine record cards held variously at the National Railway Museum, the Public Record Office, Kew, and the Scottish Record Office, Edinburgh.

H. F. Andrews, 'The Economics of Locomotive Shed Operation and Locomotive Running', a paper delivered to the Institute of Transport, 20 November 1945.

John Copsey, 'Castles' in Wales (Winter 1992 *Great Western Railway Journal*).

J. F. Harrison, Presidential Address to the Institution of Locomotive Engineers, 1961 session.

H. G. Kerry, 'The Working of a Locomotive Shed', a paper delivered to the GWR Lecture & Debating Society, 30 January 1947.

An unpublished autobiographical manuscript by W. McLagan Sir Eustace Missenden, 'Some Thoughts on Railway Motive Power', a paper delivered to the Institute of Transport, 21 November 1949.

Various issues of:

Modern Railways	*Railway World*
Railway Magazine	*SLS Journal*
Railway Observer	*Trains Illustrated*

*This is not a nostalgic book but something was lost to us with the
ending of the steam age, and the coincident explosion of
road motor transport.*

*I leave it to George Heiron to provide the caption for his beautiful
photograph entitled Happy Days!:*
*In the 1950s when country lanes were traffic-free (and free of
litter!) banks and hedgerows were sweet with wild flowers, and
glow-worms by night. Ladies were attractive like 18-year old
Shirley Tanner of Westerleigh, watching the 8am Neyland-
Paddington pass Westerleigh Jct one June morning in 1957*

1

'USING THE ENGINE AS BEST WE COULD'

The intention of this book is neither nostalgic nor sentimental, but an attempt to record something of the everyday realities of an unusual and challenging occupation, that of steam engineman. None of those I met could be described as either nostalgic or sentimental about their career but are proud of their experiences, like to talk about their time on the footplate, and relish meeting old comrades. It was a sociable occupation, one where men talked to each other, about the job, the engines, and each other.

The realities of steam operation are fast receding. Nearly 30 years have departed since steam finished on BR. Nowadays, the conditions associated with steam working seem

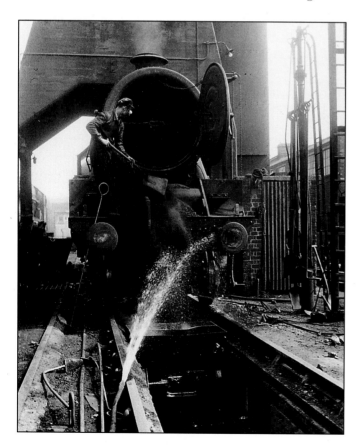

even more remote than that, given Britain's de-industrialisation and the decline of the 'smoke-stack' industries that went hand in hand with the steam-age railway. Steam bridged two ages, and nudged the world of electronic warfare, colour television and motorways.

Enginemen display some amazement at what the job had involved. Many would no doubt join Alan Corfield (Edge Hill) in musing, 'Did it really happen?' So far as large-scale steam operation on BR is concerned, and the prestige, top-notch workings with express passenger trains in particular, it's not a matter of looking back to 1968 but ten years previous to that. To all intents, top-link steam working had reduced considerably by 1961 with the influx of main line diesels, and finished during 1963, except on the Southern Region where steam literally puffed into a Waterloo Sunset in July 1967.

The end of steam operation, and the contraction in railway services and manpower associated with the Beeching Plan that placed the buffer-stops at the end of the steam age, signalled the beginning of a much greater process. This continues into the late 1990s, and has been called the collapse of work. The steam age was a labour-intensive one and, in 1949, of a total of 624,000 BR staff, 96,000 were enginemen (cleaners, firemen, drivers and motormen) and 34,000 were shed staff. They drove or helped to run nearly 20,000 steam, and 120 diesel and electric locomotives, and many hundreds of electric multiple-units. At the locomotive workshops were another 40,000 staff, engaged on new construction and overhauls. Some 27% of BR's staff were concerned with motive power which was the second largest of the railway departments. Steam generated its own traffic, too, for BR consumed some 14 million tons of locomotive coal.

'He wants to be an engine-driver when he grows up' was

'The realities of steam operation are fast receding..' This is Camden depot, London in the 1940s with a 'Jubilee' 4-6-0 over the ash-pit, and the ash-disposal plant itself in the background. A goggle-clad member of shed staff shovels hot char from the smokebox into a truck moving on rails inside the pit, and hopes that the water-spray will keep down the worst of the flying ash.
C. R. L. Coles

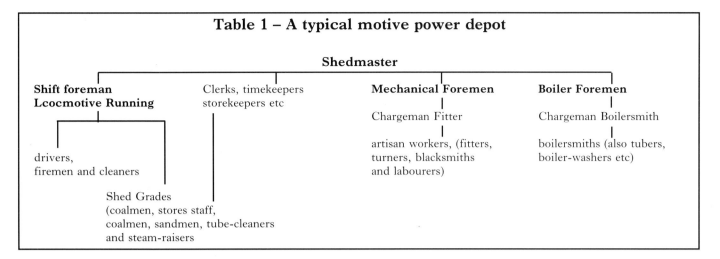

Table 1 – A typical motive power depot

	Shedmaster		
Shift foreman Lcocmotive Running	Clerks, timekeepers storekeepers etc	**Mechanical Foremen**	**Boiler Foremen**
		Chargeman Fitter	Chargeman Boilersmith
drivers, firemen and cleaners		artisan workers, (fitters, turners, blacksmiths and labourers)	boilersmiths (also tubers, boiler-washers etc)
Shed Grades (coalmen, stores staff, coalmen, sandmen, tube-cleaners and steam-raisers			

an ambition attributed to countless boys of the 1930s, 1940s, perhaps even the 1950s. In reality, the young men attracted to join the railway as engine-cleaners were unlikely to have been the recipient of the comment for these tended to be the school-cap wearing, middle-class loco-spotters at the end of a station platform. What prospects awaited the 18-year old entrant at a typical locomotive depot?

Both the occupation, and the controlling organisation, were resistant to change, even within and by the standards of a conservative industry. Shortly after Nationalisation, the Railway Executive had decided that the motive power department should be set up on its own, and divorced from the traditional control of the chief mechanical engineer's department. For each of the BR Regions, a Motive Power Superintendent was in charge, and he reported to the Chief Regional Officer and the Railway Executive.

Arguably, this was the worst reorganisation possible for it served to reinforce entrenched attitudes. Under the Motive Power Superintendent were District Motive Power Superintendents, to whom reported the locomotive inspectors, clerical staffs, and the motive power depots, in charge of which were depot shedmasters (who also ran any sub-sheds coming under their control). At each depot there were groups of workers, controlled by respective foremen. The general organisation at a medium-sized or large depot is more easily shown by a diagram - Table 1. Throughout the book references will be made to other staff at a locomotive depot, but naturally the spotlight falls on footplatemen.

The young man accepted for the post of engine-cleaner followed a rigid career pattern. It was determined by seniority which was based on the date of joining the railway; no wonder that few men today have forgotten the exact date of their starting. Some of the realities of this stage of their career and its working conditions feature in 'Feet up, Don, it's Tring'. One of the basic text-books of its day was *Locomotive Management from Cleaning to Driving*, written by two men (Hodgson and Williams) who had practical experience of the occupation. They outlined the 'calling' or 'craft' very well, explaining that the cleaner began by cleaning the least visible parts of the tender, and the locomotive in that order, pro-

gressing to the most visible, providing that 'further advancement is merited'. The cleaner needed to be 'smart, civil and obliging', they said, 'and to have his engine spotlessly clean'. This was ingenuous for taken as a whole cleaners were as high-spirited as any young men of their age. With the large numbers of cleaners on the larger sheds, some of those who have contributed to this book have made it clear that the cleaning gangs tossed a coin to see who would actually work that day, and who might sneak off.

Few cleaners have forgotten their introduction to the industry. Many recorded their experiences, but few as comprehensively as George Merry whose complete set of diaries is fortunately preserved as part of the National Collection. He started at the Bury depot of the Lancashire & Yorkshire Railway. 'Joined 25 September 1913. In first week, worked 34 hours 25min for 11/5$^1/_2$d. Shed duties, cleaned $^1/_4$ and $^1/_2$ of locomotives, including Nos 320, 1038, 834...' and so on. Cleaners were paid according to the halves or quarters of engines they cleaned.

Before 1919, and the overdue introduction of the 8hr day for railwaymen, working hours were excessive, as George Merry records. By later standards, he was soon out firing on locomotives, and by January 1914 he was working a 60-66 hour week on the Heywood pilot engine, and cleaning as well. '19 March 1914 on duty 7.45am until 7.5pm - Normanton to Aintree goods'. Throughout his career, and until his final turn as a driver in September 1960, George Merry religiously recorded the numbers of all the locomotives he had worked on, and his hours of duty.

It was little different when Ron Dansie (Neasden) started on 14 February 1938. 'I remember cleaning 'B17' No 2848 *Arsenal*, particularly because with this engine there was no foot-plating round the tender-sides! Boiler round and down, tender round and down. We tossed up for cleaning by quarters.'

The cleaner was supposed to prepare for the time he would be called upon as spare fireman and, as Hodgson and Williams counselled, he needed 'to take notice of how the fireman makes up the fire...(be) thoroughly acquainted with the different classes of oil-can, tools, fire-irons etc... give a

What the engine diagrams looked like, this example coming from Haymarket shed. It features a turn for a Haymarket 'A1' Pacific worked by two sets of Haymarket enginemen, the first set booking on at 7.30am to find the 'A1' ready prepared for them, and returning with the engine to Haymarket after a trip to Newcastle and back. The second set came on at 9.50pm, and completed their 8hr duty at 5.50am the next morning.
LE - Light Engine;
EC - Empty Carriages.

Courtesy of the
Scottish Record Office

Passenger Engine Workings Commencing on 16th September 1957

Haymarket Passenger Engines

Turn No.1	Engine prepared	Class 8P. (A.1)			Book On	Book Off	H. M.
	Haymarket E.S.	7.45 am(A)	LE.	SX.	7.30	3/30	8. 0
7.50	Edinburgh	8.30 (A)		SX.			
10.37	Newcastle	12.33pm(A)		SX.			
2.36	Edinburgh	2.40 (A)	LE.	SX.			
2.45	Haymarket E.S.						
	Engine prepared						
	Haymarket E.S.	10.5pm	LE.		9/50	5.50	8. 0
10.10	Haymarket G.L.	10.25	EC.				
10.35	Edinburgh	10.50					
1.10	Newcastle						
	do.	3.7am		MX.			
5.15	Edinburgh	5.20	LE.	MX.			
5.25	Haymarket E.S.						
	Newcastle	3.23		SUN.			
5.31	Edinburgh	5.35	LE.	SUN.			
5.40	Haymarket E.S.						

(A) Does not apply on 24th, 25th, 26th December,
3rd, 4th 7th April and 23rd, 26th May

helping hand to driver or fireman...watch the washer-out...sweeping of tubes', as well as perhaps assisting as a fitter's labourer.

Once familiar with locomotives, their components and operation, and with firing duties, the cleaner was expected to undergo an oral examination regarding railway rules and regulations, and, on passing, he became a spare fireman or passed cleaner and then received his rule-book. With experience on pilot-engines and working goods trains he was considered to have knowledge of the rules and regulations and, as Hodgson and Williams had it, '(to be) acquainted with the road, signals and gradients'.

Having gained promotion to the grade of fireman, there followed the process of learning about the locomotives themselves and train working, with progression through the hierarchy of firing turns involving pilot work, shunting, local goods, main line goods, local passenger, general passenger, and express passenger duties. It was a matter of learning by example, the onus for which fell upon the driver, provided that those worthies were co-operative. That was where the Mutual Improvement Class movement was so important, see 'A hotter place ye couldna be'. The principle is simply stated by Phil Bassett (Nine Elms): 'Only by experience could you master the job'. Eligibility for promotion was determined by the completion of a stated number of firing turns. Continuation as an engineman was conditioned by sight tests, and fears of deteriorating eyesight were always present.

The examinations for passing-out firemen were an art-form. Alan Vickery (Landore): 'There were two stages in the exam: practical, and rules and regulations, the latter (on the GWR and Western Region) being conducted at Swindon. For the practical, I was examined by Inspector Albert Poo-ley, and worked a local job to Margam and back to Neath. Then there were questions in the rest-room - and these included trick questions - repairs that couldn't be made and so on. You had to be prepared for these.' Don Buckley: 'At Edge Hill in the postwar years, there had been so little promotion that it was 1960 before Passed Firemen were being turned out regularly. When it was my turn, I sat shivering at the depot. I was examined by an inspector from Crewe, one of the nicest men possible, and he soon put me at ease. The questions covered rules and regulations, working the locomotive and the function of its component-parts, failures etc. Then lunch - "do you want to go somewhere, or have a working lunch?" At the end, he walked away, saying, "See you tomorrow morning on the Birmingham express passenger working." That was his way of telling you that you had passed'.

This was a great moment for a fireman, given that progress in the job was often so slow. To John Morgan (King's Cross): 'The brass cap-badge not only proved that you had done so many firing turns - you had paid in blood for it.' Len Glasspool (Barrow Rd): 'It took 17 years to become a fireman, and ten years for a fireman to get on top money.' Having once got to the Top Link men stayed there, by virtue of seniority. Len continues: 'A lot of men were taken on once the eight-hour day came in 1919. Many had lengthy innings as drivers. On our mileage turns to Leeds, Harry Huntley had been there for 17 years, Fred Barnett - a real gentleman - for 20.'

Progression through to promotion meant 'passing through the Links'. What did that mean, and what was the Top Link, anyway?

The diagrams for locomotives influenced the men's workings. The train service had developed to meet traffic require-ments, and motive power had to be provided to work those trains. So locomotive diagrams were produced, balancing outward with suitable return workings as far as possible, these taking into account the rosters for enginemen. The old principle of 'one engine, one set of men' had largely vanished by BR days because, given the restriction of enginemen's turns to eight hours or so, it was more economic to keep an engine at work as long as possible, beyond the scheduled time allotted to a crew. Some examples are given of engine and men's workings for a depot with express passenger work. These are from Haymarket shed, Edinburgh, which tended towards the old-fashioned system of double-shifting (else-where sometimes referred to as double-manning), just two sets of men regularly working one engine. In this case, the view was that if a limited number of enginemen were involved with each locomotive, as compared to common-user locomotives - see 'The Talk of the Line' - there was a greater incentive for engines to be handled carefully, and for their mechanical faults to be reported. That principle may be debatable, if experience at Bristol Barrow Road and on the Great Eastern Line is anything to go by.

The clerks in the timing and diagramming departments needed to deploy some ingenuity when drawing up or alter-ing locomotive diagrams and men's rosters. They had to know whether a particular depot possessed suitable motive power, and if the men at that shed who might work the engine diagram had the requisite route-knowledge - see 'When I start, dig in!'

The principle was always that a driver 'signed for the road'. That meant that he had provided an inspector with satisfac-tory answers to questions regarding all aspects of train work-ing over a particular route - the position of signals, the track layout, gradients, loops and sidings etc and gradients. He then signed his 'route card' appropriately. That knowledge had to be maintained. So far as the depot was concerned, it needed to be allocated turns that would maintain the crews' route-knowledge. For instance, despite the loss of the rest of their lodging turns to Swansea in the mid-1950s, Old Oak Common retained one weekdays' turn - see 'When I start, dig in!'. If a driver's 'knowledge' lapsed, he was required to refresh it by riding over the route on an engine. In the case of a depot being allocated a working over a 'new' route, there was a route-learning exercise to 'learn the road' and drivers traversed the route in an inspection saloon with an engine propelling at the rear.

By allocating an individual train working to enginemen as part of their turn of duty, the diagramming clerks had to match the class of train - local goods or express passenger, for instance - with appropriate enginemen, appropriate, that is, in terms of their seniority - their position on the ladder that led from shunting to express passenger work.

At any one particular depot, enginemen were arranged according to their grades, in Links, each of which was des-ignated by number, with 'No 1' usually at the top. The Links tended to be arranged according to groups of services or, less

often, geographically. Top of that list were the express pas-senger trains covered by the shed's engines - assuming that the depot had such workings, and probably the majority didn't - hence Top Link. Within each Link, there were a set number of men, usually a dozen or so, and so within the Link there were particular turns for daily or two-day rosters. So each set of men went through the run of turns allotted to their Link, and might encounter the same turn every 24 weeks, for instance. At Polmadie, and no doubt elsewhere, there was a saying: 'Taking 12 railways, there are on average 12 Links at each of the sheds, each made up of 12 men. Of these, four are experts, four are in it for the money, and four never should have been there.'

In the Top Link workings featured in *Elite Steam*, there is much talk of 'double-home workings'. Single-home work-ings are not mentioned but the term meant that the men fin-ished the duty and took their rest at their home depot. When they worked to another location, and lodged there, this was described as a double-home working, that is, they took rest away from home, and returned with a balancing working the next day.

The lodging turns in the Top Link paid well. Although that was obviously one of the main attractions for the young cleaners starting their career on the footplate, in all fairness it was only part of the story. Alan Corfield (Edge Hill): 'When you joined, the Top Link was your aspiration'. Don Buckley (Edge Hill): 'With the double-home workings, you had two trips a week. That was where everyone wanted to be. Once main line engines were allowed to run through from Liverpool Riverside to Euston, these turns were up to eight hours but worth 12 hours' pay. That was a goal for a young fireman.'

Lodging turns were usually voluntary - see 'Respected but not loved', and many men did not wish to be away from home overnight, and so declined to volunteer. In the late 1940s, men at one East Coast depot were not prepared to accept lodging turns, and the depot accordingly lost work. John Morgan (Kings Cross) comments: 'As a result, they wouldn't talk to the men from other depots who were on the lodging turns. But even within my depot there was friction between men in the non-lodge and lodge links, the latter being dep-recated as "lodging bastards". Men wouldn't talk to each other'.

Some of the out and home jobs for an engine and men were onerous, such as the Paddington-Shrewsbury working for an Old Oak 'Castle' - see 'When I start, dig in.' This conjunc-tion was unusual. In the 1950s, the longest single day's mileage for an express steam locomotive was probably the 401 miles of the summer 'Royal Scot' as worked by a Pol-madie 'Duchess' in the mid-1950s, or the corresponding East Coast working for a Kings Cross or Haymarket 'A4' between Kings Cross and Edinburgh. In each case, the engine was remanned en route. Later, there was a working for a Strat-ford 'Britannia' which took in over 500 miles in 24 hours: Liverpool St-Parkeston Quay; from there to Sheffield and back with the Liverpool boat train, and returning to London overnight. There was remanning en route. In practice, higher mileages were achieved by some locomotives, particularly when Pacifics from Kings Cross shed deputised for diesels and worked out with the 10am 'Flying Scotsman' to Newcastle, to return with the 5pm Newcastle-Kings Cross - a total of 536 miles in 12hr. Again, the engine was remanned.

The practice of seniority was frequently criticised on the grounds that it encouraged the retention of older drivers in the highest links solely because of their 'seniority', their official date of joining. Surely, it was argued, competence should be the yardstick and younger men given a chance. Phil Bassett (Nine Elms): 'You could argue both ways, as you were progressing up the tree you were all for seniority but as a passed fireman and off the main line you were critical of the senior men.'

The hierarchical system was nonetheless generally accepted. It became distorted when large numbers of men were taken on, principally during the two world wars, and following introduction of the 8hr day. Those who joined in 1918/9 passed out as drivers in 1937 or so, but those taken on a couple of years later not until the later years of the war. As some clue to the manning levels, in 1938 ASLE&F membership had totalled 53,000, by 1944 it was 69,000, and it increased further in 1946 to 72,000.

Promotion also depended on the situation of a particular shed, or the practice of the controlling Region. Some young men progressed relatively fast to become drivers at sheds such as Bushbury where Ron Brazier had been taken on in 1940. He had ten years as a top-link fireman, became a driver in 1952, and was a Top Link driver by the late 1950s. On the GWR and Western Region it was possible to transfer to other depots to gain promotion but that was not the case elsewhere. It was then a matter of dead men's shoes - waiting for older men to retire so that everyone could move up to the next link.

The occupation of engineman ran in some families. One LMR driver was one of five sons whose father was himself a driver, then a senior driver, and finally a running shift foreman. 'We were all put on the railway, there wasn't a choice. If you had a relation on the railway, you had a chance.' Some families were strongly represented at depots, as Don Flook (Barrow Rd) explains: 'It was typical of many British locosheds of the period with its sense of family. I was a fitter, one of three whose fathers were drivers at the shed. There were staff whose family had worked on the Somerset & Dorset Joint Line, or had themselves started there. The S&D sheds came under Barrow Road.' Because locomotive depots often had their own enclaves - see 'Living with the aristocracy' and also 'In a hotter place ye couldna be' - and disregarding for a moment customary causes for resentment, the depot was more generally akin to a large family. R. Brazier (Bushbury): 'We were all very good mates - you had to be to work the job right.'

That family feeling was sometimes a response to the attitudes of the outside world towards railwaymen in general, and enginemen in particular. Willie McLagan (Polmadie):

'On my father's side they were mostly in the railways and on my mother's side in engineering. My father was a driver at Polmadie. I began as an apprentice with a firm of engineers but gave it up, and went down to Polmadie shed to ask for a job there, and was taken on as a cleaner. Uncle Will on my mother's side took a fit and went on about the waste of education and skill to join such an ignorant shower as railwaymen; in his view they were an uneducated lot. My father said, "I hope you know what you're letting yourself in for!" He based his comment on his hard struggles from the bad, old days of 1905 onwards.'

Those 'bad, old days' were characterised by the dominance of the running foremen who effectively controlled promotion, sometimes corruptly, countenanced the excessive hours being worked, and exacted fines for claimed misdemeanours. No proper recognition was given to enginemen for their skills. Enginemen rightly felt that they were craftsmen, and the unions worked hard to change conditions. The Associated Society of Locomotive Engineers & Firemen upheld the case for craft unionism as compared with the industrial unionism represented by the National Union of Railwaymen. The NUR also represented footplatemen, and in 1955 claimed 17,000 footplatemen members, although some men were members of both unions. Mention of 1955 raises the matter of the footplate strike called by the ASLE&F that year. Its occurrence generated ill-feeling between members of the two unions at personal, depot and national levels. Some of that discord lingered into recent years.

Union membership was - and remains - a matter of great pride. Although there were allegations of militancy at some depots, vehemently-held opinions did not necessarily equate with lack of co-operation, as 'In a hotter place ye couldna be' makes clear. In representing the workplace level in negotiation between the unions collectively and management, the role of the Local Departmental Committees (LDCs) should not be underestimated. They worked towards resolution of such matters as the arrangement of working hours including depot rostering, and issues involving meal breaks and holidays.

Some enginemen involved themselves with the wider community. Many served as councillors on local councils, and generally they represented the Labour Party. Driver Charlie Simmons of Kings Cross began his career in Great Northern Railway days. He was twice Mayor of Finsbury, then leader of the Council, a governor of the board controlling two local hospitals, and a JP. His undoubted achievement was not exceptional. Senior drivers, particularly those on the lucrative mileage turns, often became property-owners in a modest way, with a couple of houses for letting, or a shop which might be run by their wives or by another member of the family.

Never mind the long hours, irregular starting-times and frequent night-work, the conditions of work were always arduous. The lodgings for the men on double-home workings were frequently appalling - 'the sheets were often warm from the last man'. The railway hostels were preferable, such as they were in prewar years. Men took their own food with them and cooked meals in the hostel. Postwar, the hostels were increased in number.

Mostly they relied on the 'Box' or snap-tin - a metal tin - that had been packed up with food at home. The contents might be half-a-loaf of bread, a hunk of cheese and a bottle of tea without milk or sugar. Meals were frequently snatched anywhere convenient, whatever the regulations said about taking meal-breaks at particular times. In the Leicester Central mess-room, as Ron Dansie and his mate took their personal needs' break 'mice ran along the pipes.' Willie McLagan (Polmadie): 'The pattern of irregular and hurried meals and shifts meant that stomach ulcers were a major problem. I spent a lot of time visiting colleagues in hospital.'

Ulcers and deafness were perhaps the greatest occupational hazards, and additional to injuries inflicted at what was in any case a dangerous place of work, on and off the engines. Fred Barral (Clacton): 'We were working a "B17" once. The regulator was stiff, and my driver got on the "piano-stool" that served as a seat on these engines. He yanked at the regulator, fell back and, although I caught him in my arms, he had knocked himself out.' The steam locomotive was a solid and unyielding machine that often responded only to brutal methods. Phil Bassett: 'One day at Nine Elms, the firehole

door had jammed shut on an engine in steam. In an effort to cool it and for the metal to contract, we sprayed water on the door to produce clouds of steam, and then whacked it with a sledge-hammer.' Brutal methods did not produce the best results when it came to driving an engine.

The incidence of accidents and their effect on enginemen deserves a book to itself. Those involved in accidents seldom forgot them. They tended to relive the moments leading to the incident, and to rehearse their explanation of what had caused it. Alan Vickery (Landore) perhaps sums up most men's philosophy: 'In 40 or so years on the footplate, if an engineman had not experienced an accident of some sort, he was either a bloody fool or a genius'.

Enginemen were usually intrigued with other people's reactions to their working conditions. A first-hand view was possible in an age when people were not infrequently invited up on the footplate to ride with them. Ted Abear (Old Oak):

The driver and fireman worked closely although their relationship might not always be harmonious...
This is another scene from Camden shed, showing a fireman with the 'bag' in the tender, and the driver ready to shut the valve of the water column (and being distracted by the photographer!).
C. R. L. Coles

Enginemen and shed staff converse at Camden in the mid-1950s. The driver of a 'Royal Scot' is oiling round. Look at the working environment with the heaps of ash, and spilled coal. This depot was frequently criticised by the local authority for smoke emission - but this was inseparable from the steam engine.

C. R. L. Coles

On Saturday night in 1958 my driver, Arthur Evans and I were booked to work a Paddington-Pembroke Dock special as far as Cardiff. We had a 'Grange' as a pilot. When we hooked on at Paddington, we found that it was a naval special, with a ship's company going to pick up their ship. An officer came up to our engine and said that two of the stokers wanted a ride. One came on our engine, No 5029 *Nunney Castle*, the other on the 'Grange'. As we went through Reading, the stoker asked me, 'Is it always like this? I've never fired on a coal-burner, how can you manage with all this rock and roll? Looking back, the driver on the 'Grange' shook his fist at us by way of a challenge and Arthur let the 'Castle' out. 'Hark at the noise', said the stoker, 'I've never had an experience like this!' After the passage of the Severn Tunnel, he couldn't wait to get off at Cardiff.

Working conditions were much worse in the early postwar years, for reasons explained in 'A tale of burnished buffers'. The railway was labour-intensive, and as the industry steadily became uncompetitive in the labour market during the late 1940s many of the personnel employed were of doubtful quality. Alan Vickery and Bruce Joyce (Landore): 'Some enginemen were ignorant - as thick as two short planks. 70% probably had no interest in the job. At that time, on the railway in general there was widespread thieving and pilfering of loaded wagons, and at goods depots'.

Drivers were self-evidently central to the motive power organisation. To some extent, this book is biased in the sense that, with one or two notable exceptions, the evidence presented relies strongly on those who were firemen during the final days of steam rather than the drivers of the time. Quite simply, the majority of their drivers are no more. Most formed part of the major intake that had occurred after World War 1. Views vary. Drivers were variously seen: favourably as 'good, old boys', or unfavourably in a variety of terms, mostly unprintable. As John Morgan (Kings Cross) points out: 'A lot had to do with precedent. If they had been badly treated themselves as firemen then that affected their attitude as drivers. They were heavy-handed.' Those who had been economical with coal as firemen were 'light' when it came to their handling of engines as a driver, and accordingly were considerate towards fireman.

Some drivers were plain arrogant or obtuse. Phil Bassett (Nine Elms): 'I well remember one day, booking on, only to find that I was firing to an immaculately dressed driver who regarded all firemen as rubbish. He called me not by my name but 'fireman'. It was Christmas week. At 60mph, with the regulator in the roof, he pulled out a packet of cigars, and took off the wrapper. "Fireman, do you smoke cigars?" 'Yes.' "Well, this won't be one of those occasions". John Morgan (Kings Cross): 'One driver I fired to said to me. "I won't let you drive - you'll learn by watching me. One day you'll be allowed to be a driver. The next day, he did let me have a spell driving. The day after, he said: "You made quite a good job of it - my wrist was giving trouble.'

Don Buckley (Edge Hill) booked on one day, found the engine - a 'Jubilee' - and got up on the tender. The driver was 'Gentleman Bill'. As he put his coat in the locker on the engine he looked up at me - 'Who are you?' Ignor-

Once serviced, the engines passed 'on shed' for stabling, and the interiors of the buildings were memorable, sometimes awe-inspiring:

(Right)
Light and shade in one of Old Oak Common's roundhouses. This finely judged picture won Lewis Coles First Prize in the Ian Allan 1949 Photographic Competition. The nearest engine is No 6846 Ruckley Grange *- 'Kings' and 'Castles' lurk in the gloom on the opposite side of the turntable.*

(Below)
A prewar study of Willesden's roundhouse with two 'Jubilee' 4-6-0s, a Hughes 2-6-0 and an LMS '4F' 0-6-0.
C. R. L. Coles

(Left)
Willesden shed sprawled across a wide area, and as with many other steam depots, the mechanical coaling plant pinpointed the site for miles.
C. R. L. Coles

(Right)
Inside Kings Cross shed are two household names - 'A4' Mallard *and 'V2'* Green Arrow, *happily both now preserved. The 'cod's mouth' of the 'A4' is open for access to the smokebox.*
C. R. L. Coles

ing my answer, 'Gentleman Bill' called over to the foreman, "Is he all right?" Yes, was the answer. Bill retorted, "I'll tell you tomorrow what I think" That sort of attitude manifested itself in another form of contemptuousness, the driver who drew a chalk line down the boiler backhead and the length of the footplate. That's your side, fireman, this is mine was the attitude.

Many of the older men were characters to the point of being eccentric. Don Buckley (Edge Hill): 'I fired to a driver who every day took a lump of coal off the tender . He then expertly split it with a $^{7}/_{8}$in spanner into slices, and put these into his jacket to take home for the kitchen fire.'

Some were unhappy at working with diesel or electric locomotives. Driver Murphy at Birkenhead Mollington St was one. 'He hated the sight of diesels and continued to come to work in his steam overalls. He was fearless. Towards the end of steam we were working the Ellesmere Port-Liversedge oil-tanker train with a "9F". Running at 60mph across Chat Moss near Manchester, he calmly opened the side-door and clambered partway down the steps to remove a piece of newspaper. "It's been annoying me for miles", he said.

Peculiarities apart, the professionalism of many of the older drivers is a topic that recurs frequently when talking to enginemen. To Don Buckley (Edge Hill): 'It was always said that drivers never got paid for what they knew, and what they did. All those crack passenger trains with 400-600 people aboard. The drivers were no different to airline pilots.'

Many of the firemen marvelled at the ability of the 'good, old boys' to know exactly where they were on the line, whatever the weather conditions. R. Brazier (Bushbury): 'I fired to Harry Oakley, up and down to London on the 2hr trains, on time, never mind the fog. He knew exactly where to look out for signals, only then did he put his head out of the cab window'. Generally, drivers handled their engines by the 'feel of it' rather than by text-book instruction, with differing results.

The image of lantern-jawed, self-confident drivers takes a knock when listening to firemen's accounts. Alan Vickery

and Bruce Joyce (Landore): 'Some drivers were as nervous as kittens, some had no nerve in their bodies, others would talk about everything but railways. Some showed concern unless the water-level was well up in the gauge-glass, or else displayed their lack of confidence, asking the fireman for instance, "do you want the blower on?"'.

Many were quite the opposite, and in John Morgan's experience at Kings Cross shed 'some drivers were always double-checking, and told you when to fire, or to put on the injector'. Firemen took exception to instructions of this sort. Dennis Webb (Clacton): 'One driver infuriated firemen by calling everyone, irrespective of their names, "Charlie". This was usually linked to a command, such as "Don't put any more (coal) on, Charlie!" He always interfered, and wouldn't leave the fireman to his own devices'. Other drivers reacted to criticism of unpunctuality - when Control-logs had indicated 'Time lost to Loco' - by blaming the fireman.

All told, despite the hardships and frustrations, many of those who subsequently left the railway regard their time as a steam engineman as does N. P. Bravery (Neasden): 'the best job I ever had. Given half a chance I would go back to those days again'. Of those who went on to become drivers working with diesel or electric traction, their attitude to steam locomotives is best summed up by Dennis Webb (Clacton): 'We had to create our own power, to make the engine work, and to use the engine as best we could. Half the battle was knowing the road'.

2

THROWING DOWN THE GAUNTLET
– the Bushbury 'Jubilees'

In the ranks of Elite Steam, West Coast enthusiasts would surely agree that the Bushbury 'Jubilees' were near the top of the list. But their election to the elite was not assured. In the absence of Class '7' motive power, one Bushbury shedmaster challenged the depot's enginemen to show their mettle with the 'Jubilees'. Here's how they responded.

To my mind, there were few more impressive steam age spectacles than a well-cleaned LMS 'Jubilee' raising the echoes at the head of an express train. On the Western Division of the London Midland Region, 'Jubilees' were regularly to be found at the head of the Euston-Birmingham-Wolverhampton expresses - and the really clean ones came from Bushbury.

A fast service between the capital, the second city and the ancient borough of Wolverhampton dates back to the first decade of the 20th century, and the London and North Western Railway. By 1905, there were four two-hour trains each way between Euston and Birmingham, booked non-stop at an average speed of 56.5 mph over the 113 miles.

Soon after Grouping, the LMS introduced its standard Compounds to the Birmingham two-hour trains and on these workings their maximum tare load was 270 tons. The North Western men from Bushbury (Wolverhampton) and

Camden sheds obtained some good performances from the Compounds on the two-hour expresses although it was regarded as exacting work for men and machines alike.

Apart from stops inserted at Coventry in the schedules of the non-stops, by 1933 the Compounds also had to cope with an additional stop at Willesden Junction on the 4.50pm up two-hour train from Birmingham. Later known as the 'Patriots', the 'Rebuilt Claughton' '5X' 4-6-0s were beginning to appear and these could be loaded to 350 tons on the two-hour trains. By the late summer of 1934, the first Stanier taper-boilered '5Xs', Nos 5552-6, were allocated to Bushbury and Aston sheds and displaced Compounds on the fast Birmingham services. That autumn, dynamometer car trials were conducted between Wolverhampton and Euston with a 'Patriot' and a 'Jubilee'. The intention was to assess the chances of accelerating the two-hour trains.

The results obtained with the 'Jubilee' were something of a disappointment. As far as the Euston-Wolverhampton service was concerned, the first five 'Jubilees' had made themselves unpopular with their problematic steaming, in part attributable to their low degree of superheating. By April 1935 - and not for the last time in this story - the Bushbury 'Jubilees' were transferred away, to be replaced by 'Patriots'.

Comparative dynamometer trials continued between Wolverhampton and Euston, pitting 'Jubilees' in original two-row and in modified three-row superheater form against 'Patriots'. This demonstrated that the 'Jubilee' with the higher degree of superheat offered some improvement over the original specification even if it was inferior in efficiency to the parallel-boilered 'Patriot'. With the winter 1935/6 timetable, the timings of the fastest Birmingham-Euston were nonetheless pared to 115 min while the 6.20pm from Birmingham reached Euston in two hours despite three intermediate stops.

Drawing on test results and running experience, a series of modifications was applied to those 'Jubilees' built at Crewe from late 1935 - numbered 5665 and above - to effect an improvement in the performance of the class. Throughout 1936/7, trials continued to be conducted between Wolverhampton and Euston with variously modified 'Jubilees', including No 5740, an example from the last series of 'Jubilees', and No 5684, fitted with a Kylchap exhaust and double chimney. Yet the 'Patriots' remained at work on the Euston-Wolverhampton service. As late as July 1938, Bushbury and Aston sheds each had seven 'Patriots' for these workings, neither Bushbury nor Aston having any 'Jubilees' on their allocations at the start of that year.

Some of the 'Jubilees'' steaming problems had been rectified but, until the end of their days, their performance could be somewhat erratic when they were not correctly handled, or had to cope with dubious coal. In the form that finally evolved with three-row superheater, redesigned and domed boiler, as well as improved draughting, 'Jubilees' were at last allocated in quantity to Bushbury and Aston sheds during March 1939. Nos 5721-3/36/40-2 went to the latter and 5719/33-5/7-9 to Bushbury. Seven of these 'Jubilees' were

(Opposite)
The only named train between Euston and Wolverhampton was the postwar 'Midlander'. Here the down express nears Bletchley on 19 May 1955, headed by 'Jubilee' 4-6-0 No 45586 Mysore. *This engine was not generally associated with Bushbury, but was allocated there from February-July 1955, and had been loaned to the shed in the autumn of 1952.*
D. M. C. Hepburne-Scott/Rail Archive Stephenson

(Above)
What on earth is a 'Castle' doing in this chapter? Pictures of the environs of Bushbury shed are not that common and here it is photographed from the road overbridge, at a time when Birkenhead-Wolverhampton-Paddington trains such as this one were being diverted from their normal route. The date is 29 November 1953, and the engine is 'Castle' 4-6-0 No 5015 Kingswear Castle.
F. W. Shuttleworth

to be associated with Bushbury over most of the next 20 years. These prewar difficulties with the 'Jubilees' have been recounted to provide a perspective against which to judge their fine and generally consistent work during the mid and late 1950s.

An LNWR depot dating from 1859, Bushbury was located some 1½ miles north of Wolverhampton. The shed building was reconstructed in 1883 and was a brick-built structure with eight stabling roads. One dominant feature of the northern part of the site was the old water-tower which was condemned as unsafe in BR days. During the LMS period the depot was modernised by the provision of mechanised coaling and ash disposal facilities, and a 70ft turntable. During World War 2, a canteen building was provided at the southern end of the site.

Bushbury was a railway community, grouped around the overbridge beyond the divergence of the Stour Valley and Grand Junction lines, the most notable non-railway building being the Oxley Arms public house - if one discounts the local morgue! There were two sets of railway cottages, a dozen or so for enginemen, and another row near the shed coaling-plant, these being occupied by permanent way staff. Later, a hostel was provided for enginemen working to Wolverhampton on lodging turns. In 1956, Bushbury gained a British Railways Staff Association social club which sur-

(Left)
Camden bank and No 45742 Connaught - *by this time with single chimney - raises the echoes in true 'Jubilee' style on 3 October 1959 with the 4.25pm down for Wolverhampton, routed via Northampton. The smokebox door carries the train reporting number W125 and, sadly, a decline in cleaning standards is obvious.*
R. C. Riley

(Below)
A change from all those 'Jubilees'! Rebuilt 'Patriot' No 45531 Sir Frederick Harrison *was allocated to Bushbury when painted in what was unkindly described by some as 'cesspool' green. It is working with a set of LMS design coaches - including articulated vehicles of the 1939/40 'Coronation Scot' stock - in the similarly experimental BR plum and spilt milk livery. The date is 1948.*
C. R. L. Coles

vives as one of the few reminders of the concentration of railway families in the locality.

Bushbury shed's allocation was never more than some 60 engines and, by the late 1940s, was down to 40 or so, comprising express power for the London trains, a few local passenger tank engines, as well as shunting pilots and goods engines for trip workings. Under the LMS, Bushbury was coded 3B and came under the control of the neighbouring Bescot depot. This code was applicable until June 1960 when Bushbury was transferred to the Saltley district, and became 21C. For its last three years of life (1963-5), the depot was no more than a sub-shed (coded 2K) in the merged Tyseley and Saltley districts. By this time, its most prestigious engines were a trio of 'Black Fives' and a couple of LNWR 'Super D' 0-8-0s, and the depot played no direct part in providing motive power for the Wolverhampton-Euston trains.

The period on either side of Nationalisation saw little change from the slough of the later war years although locomotives and set of coaches painted in experimental BR liveries were used during 1948/9 on the Euston-Wolverhampton trains. By then, Bushbury had a mixed allocation of '5X' and '6' 4-6-0s. When J. Hurley came to Bushbury as a passed cleaner early in 1950, the shed had rebuilt 'Patriots', Nos 45531 *Sir Frederick Harrison* and 45540 *Sir Robert Turnbull* in the experimental apple-green livery, and LMS black-liveried Nos 45521 *Rhyl*, 45525 *Colwyn Bay*, 45526 *Morecambe & Heysham* and 45534 *E. Tootal Broadhurst*. Loads were often considerably increased from prewar days. For a '5X' or '6', a train of 400 tons-plus represented a tough proposition, made worse by the imposition of speed restrictions - and inferior train regulation at times, both features that were less prevalent in the late 1930s.

Minor retimings were made to a couple of Euston-Wolverhampton trains in the summer 1950 timetable, at a time when there was publicly expressed dissatisfaction with the service. Pressure from Midlands' civic bodies and businessmen for an improved service between London and Birmingham drew a guarded promise from the Railway Executive that a target of 130min with one stop was in prospect, but not before the summer of 1951. Caution on the part of the authorities was justified because the availability of the Class '6s' was none too good, and the 'Jubilees' played a major part in the Top

The date is 1951 and the down 'Midlander' is passing Harrow & Wealdstone behind No 45738 Samson *which was on Bushbury's allocation from Period 7|51, having been at the shed for a brief period before World War 2.*

This engine was one of those that came to Bushbury in mid-1951, in replacement of the 'Royal Scots' which had been transferred to work the Euston-Wolverhampton expresses in the winter 1950/1 timetable.

C. R. L. Coles

Link duties. Camden shed was also involved in working the service but generally provided 'Royal Scots' or rebuilt 'Patriots' for its turns. J. Hurley recalls: 'The Camden men weren't above gloating over their good fortune to the Bushbury men.'

In early September 1950, Bushbury's allocation of express engines comprised the following 'Jubilees':

45703 *Thunderer*	45726 *Vindictive*
45718 *Dreadnought*	45733 *Novelty*
45722 *Defence*	45741 *Leinster*
45724 *Warspite*	45742 *Connaught*

Change came more quickly than forecast by the Railway Executive, with effect from the winter 1950/1 timetable. The 8.5am SX Euston-Wolverhampton and 10.55am return were new services, trains at these times not having featured in the prewar timetables. The former 11.25am down was accelerated by 13min and retimed to leave at 12.30pm, except on Saturdays when it kept its original departure time. The new 10.55am up and the existing 5.45pm down were distinguished by the name 'Midlander', the train set on this return

working having the added distinction of liquid soap and towels in the lavatories of the coaches! Re-routed via Northampton, the 4.35pm down now made additional stops, to pick-up at Watford Junction, and to set-down passengers at Rugby.

The operating authorities seemingly felt that Class '5X' motive power, as represented by the 'Jubilees' (they were promoted to Class '6' from January 1951), was unable to maintain the far from difficult schedules in the 1950/1 timetable. For the improved service, Class '7' 'Royal Scots' were drafted to Bushbury, the process being completed by January 1951. No 46140 *The King's Royal Rifle Corps*

worked the inaugural up 'Midlander' of 25 September 1950. The displaced 'Jubilees' went principally to Crewe North and Carlisle Upperby depots. For the record, the incoming 'Scots' were Nos 46110/34/40/8/51/8/63/5. Of these, No 46110 *Grenadier Guardsman* was in badly rundown condition, and unrebuilt. The improvements turned out to be short-lived as a shortage of coal during early 1951 led to the suspension of a number of Euston-Wolverhampton trains.

The shed rumour had it that a couple of 'Princess Royals' were to be allocated to Bushbury for the improved services. With their non-appearance, the morale of Bushbury enginemen suffered and the LDC complained to the authorities. J. Hurley remembers sitting in the shed canteen early in 1951 when a Top Link driver made clear his dissatisfaction to the shedmaster.

He was listened to patiently. The shedmaster's response was to the point. 'Do you want the shed to lose the London jobs?' There was no reply. The boss warmed to his theme, telling the drivers that unless they shut up and kept time on the London service, Bushbury would lose work to Monument Lane or Aston sheds. Admonishment now changed to flattery. 'Why', the shedmaster said, 'anyone could run the London expresses with a "Lizzie" (a 'Princess Royal') but it takes dedicated and experienced men to time the jobs with a "Jubilee" - and you've proved you can do it!' 'Put your fingers up to the Camden men - Bushbury men can do the job with a "Jubilee"'. With this he turned on his heel and walked

Past Carpenders Park on 3 August 1957 come Monument Lane Compound No 40936 and Bushbury's 'Jubilee' No 45709 Implacable with what is probably the Saturday counterpart of the down 'Midlander'. No 45709 is paired with a Fowler tender. By 1957, the Compounds were coming near to the end of their time as pilots on Western Division expresses.
C. R. L. Coles

out of the canteen. The shedmaster had thrown down the gauntlet, and the Bushbury enginemen responded accordingly.

As promised by the Railway Executive, the summer 1951 timetable brought accelerations to the Euston-Wolverhampton service as from 2 July, including 130min timings between Euston and Birmingham (including Coventry stops) for the 12.40, 2.15, 5.45 and 6.55pm down, and the 7.50, 9.55, 10.55 and 11.55am and 3.55pm up from Wolverhampton. Overall journey times were upwards from a minimum of 160 min. The speeding-up surprisingly coincided with the transfer away of the 'Scots' from Bushbury, in exchange for 'Jubilees'. In the four weeks ending 7 July 1951 the shed received Nos 45688, 45703/33/4/7/8/41/2.

Further retimings came with the winter 1951/2 timetable but with no reduction to the fastest timings. Users of the service had to wait until the summer 1953 service, with the introduction of a new 8.50am SX Euston-Wolverhampton, featuring a non-stop run from Watford Junction to Birm-

No 45740 Munster *near Chelmscote bridge with a Birmingham-Euston express on 16 October 1955.*
D. M. C. Hepburne-Scott/Rail Archive Stephenson

(Below)
Double-chimneyed No 45742 Connaught *creates a purposeful picture at the head of a Wolverhampton-Euston express near Tring on 20 April 1952. Excellent performances were being reported with this engine at this time and respected commentator, R. A. H. Weight, reported it as 'being quite master of the job' on 13/14 coach trains he had timed between Euston and Birmingham.*
C. R. L. Coles

ingham New Street, at an average speed of 60.8 mph. Except on Saturdays, there were better than even-time average speeds - 94 miles in 93min - for the Euston-Coventry (and vice versa) runs of the 12.50, 2.20, 5.50 'Midlander' and 6.50pm down. Just under an average speed of 60 mph were the Coventry-Euston bookings, again Saturdays excepted, of the 8.30, 11.30am, and 12.30, 2.30 and 4.30pm ex-New Street.

At last, Birmingham had regained the two-hour schedules of prewar days to/from Euston. The Railway Executive con-gratulated itself that 'a prewar service at comparable speed had been restored for the first time since the War'. One other development was the alteration of departure times to provide 'clockface' times of 30min past the hour up from Birmingham and 50min down from Euston. There were however a few inconsistencies, and the Saturday schedules were generally expanded to allow for heavier tare loads. The winter

1953/4 timetable saw the 9.5am down re-routed via Northampton. In the winter 1954/5 timetable, the 1.55pm from Wolverhampton was accelerated to run between Rugby and Euston in 79 min for the 82$\frac{1}{2}$ miles, at an average speed of 62.7mph. At the time it had the fastest start to stop booking of any train on the LMR. On Fridays, the 1.55pm loaded more heavily and was allowed extra time.

Now began the legendary postwar heyday of the 'Jubilees' on this route. On the 'XL' timings of the two-hour trains, the 'Jubilees' were permitted to take a maximum of 350 tons tare, equal to 10 coaches of BR Standard corridor stock. If a train loaded more heavily, the driver was entitled to request an assisting engine. The result was that either a 'Black Five' was turned out, or, during the early/mid 1950s, a Compound 4-4-0, often one of the Monument Lane engines.

Apart from the steep climb out to Camden from Euston, the former London & Birmingham Railway route generally has ruling gradients of 1 in 330, but steady steaming was required on the lengthy uphill stretches to Tring in both directions, and northbound from near Willesden to Carpenders Park. 'Steaming' being an operative word with the 'Jubilees', it speaks for the standard of engines and enginemen's skills that the class did so well on the two-hour trains which from 1953-59 ran on the Euston-Wolverhampton service. Bushbury shed deserved commendation for its efforts,

The graceful lines of No 45737 Atlas *are captured by the photographer as the engine speeds a Birmingham New Street-Euston relief express towards Coventry on 28 March 1959.*
Michael Mensing

(Opposite)
A fine character study at Euston c 1953 of Driver George Lawrence of Bushbury shed and his fireman - with footplating visitor, George Green! The engine is Bushbury's No 45742 Connaught.
C. R. L. Coles

more visibly expressed by the smart external condition of its allocation, but Camden engines and men were responsible for some fine work, too.

Timekeeping on the two-hour trains varied. Valuable evidence comes from the records of K. R. Phillips who amassed a large collection of performance logs, including some remarkable performances by Bushbury engines. Commenting on the standard of steam locomotive performance south of Rugby on all Western Division expresses he was to say: 'In my experience the locomotive performance on the northbound trains was never very good, to Tring or points north......the performances I recorded on the "Jubilee" hauled Birmingham trains were of a much higher standard, although very few of them were on time by Tring or Rugby, but the 3min recovery time allowed for the Brandon slack often saved the train being late in Coventry'.

Whatever the standard of timekeeping, the 'racing pages' of the railway press were soon reporting good performances from 'Jubilees' working the accelerated trains during the summer of 1953. No 45742 *Connaught* was described by the late Cecil J. Allen as 'a star performer' in his 'Locomotive Running Past and Present' column when describing its run on the 2.20pm in the November 1953 issue of *Trains Illustrated*. By passing Rugby in an actual time of 76min from Euston, Allen commented that 'it is striking to recall that the "Coronation Scot", a formation limited to 300 tons tare tons and with Pacific haulage, in 1939 was allowed 76min for the same distance; *Connaught* has bettered the same time with a train heavier by 50 tons.' With an easy approach to the city, the train reached Coventry in 89$\frac{1}{2}$min from Euston against the 93min schedule. Overall running time to Birmingham was just 110$\frac{3}{4}$min.

At about this time, again on the 2.20pm down, A. J. Powell rode on the footplate of the same engine. Most of the work was done, he noted, 'with the main valve of the regulator only

just open and only 18-20% cut-off'. *Connaught* was, he said, 'an excellent steaming engine and very economical'. Water consumption was estimated as nearly 33 gallons/mile. No 45742 was fitted with the plain double exhaust and double chimney which it carried until late 1955.

Several outstanding performances were recorded with 'Scots' on the two-hour trains, particularly when working the Camden turn on the 1.55pm ex-Wolverhampton with its 62mph sprint up from Rugby. Even so, during 1955, C. J. Allen timed Camden 'Jubilee' No 45686 to need no more than $78\frac{1}{4}$ min from Rugby to Euston on a train of 336 tons tare, despite being worked fairly easily. Bushbury's No 45741 was at the head of the 1.55pm on a heavier train of 361 tons tare and took 74min 48sec unchecked. CJA adjudged this performance as 'one of the finest that I have ever known with a "Jubilee" hauling a load of this magnitude'. Unfortunately, the crew of No 45741 were not identified but they picked up all but $1\frac{3}{4}$min of a 6min late start from Rugby, and without the engine exceeding 82 mph.

During the mid-1950s Bushbury provided the engines for the majority of the Euston-Wolverhampton expresses. The depot had nine 'Jubilees' for five turns, one of the these requiring two engines. On weekdays in the winter 1954/5 timetable, individual workings for the 3B 'Jubilees' were as follows:

6.40am ex-Wolverhampton, back with the 2.20pm ex-Euston

7.50am ex-Wolverhampton, then 3pm Euston-Northampton, the 5.40pm to Birmingham New Street, a Birmingham-Euston parcels, and the 9am ex-Euston on Day 'B'.

9.45am ex-Wolverhampton, back with the 2.35pm ex-Euston

11.00am ex-Wolverhampton, back with the 5.50pm ex-Euston

11.55am ex-Wolverhampton, back with the 6.55pm ex-Euston

3.55pm ex-Wolverhampton, back Day 'B' with the 6.24am Watford Junction-Northampton-Birmingham

On those diagrams with short turn-rounds in London the engines were serviced at Euston where they used the turntable alongside Platforms 14/15 on the western side of the terminus. During their stop, local staff brought forward the coal in the tender. When the LMR and SR diesel locomotives came to be used on the route in the mid/late 1950s their usual diagram covered return trips to Wolverhampton, and to Birmingham on the same day.

In the Bushbury Top Link there were 12 turns, eight covering the Wolverhampton-Euston expresses, the remainder, local passenger workings, to Burton-on-Trent and Coventry. Two of the London turns involved lodging at Camden, the remainder were out and back workings. The lodging turns were up on the 6.40am ex-Wolverhampton, the crew having booked on at 5am to prepare their engine which returned from Euston on the 2.20pm down in the hands of another set of Bushbury men. Having booked off at Camden, the crew on the 5am turn returned to Wolverhampton with the next day's 6.24am Watford Junction-Birmingham New St stopping train - to complete 'a diabolical turn', in R. Brazier's recollection.

Camden shed (1B) had just one duty on the service, Saturdays excepted. One of its 'Jubilees' worked the 8.50am from Euston, to return with the 1.55pm from Wolverhampton; after no more than a 40min interval at New St, the Camden crew off the 8.50am down returned south with the Bushbury 'Jubilee' working the up 'Midlander'. Previous to the winter 1954/5 timetable, 1B had covered the 5.50pm down, and the 7.50am up the next day. Weekend turns were somewhat different for both Bushbury and Camden.

An out and back journey of some 250 miles may be compared unfavourably with the two return trips expected from 'Britannias' working the Liverpool Street-Norwich express service. In practical terms though the out and back journeys on the Wolverhampton expresses were preferable to the complicated cyclical workings with which the London Midland Region so often came unstuck. These out and back workings for engine and men were part of Bushbury's success with the 'Jubilees'. 'Engines in the Top Link were generally handled by the same crew there and back for a day's work. It paid crews to look after their engines', comments J. Hurley. On these mileage turns, the crews were paid the equivalent of $16\frac{1}{2}$hr for their 250-mile round trip.

During the mid-1950s, the Bushbury Top Link included Drivers Jack 'Dickie' Bird, Bill Burgess, Albert Griffith, George Lawrence, Frank Leary, Ted Oakley, 'Tommy' Potter, Tom Radford, Bill Ryman, Robin Shotton, Arthur Smith, George 'Gunboat' Smith, George 'Sausage' Smith and his brother Bob, and Ernie Upton. R. Brazier started on the railway in 1940 and spent ten years in Bushbury's Top Link - usually working with Driver Ted Oakley, remembered as 'a fine chap' - until promoted as a driver in 1952. He had progressed to the London turns before the fast trains were withdrawn in November 1959, demonstrating that Bushbury offered its enginemen much faster promotion than was customary at most other sheds.

George Lawrence is a well-remembered Bushbury driver. He had a caravan at Abersoch and a couple of properties in Wolverhampton. George Green remembers him saying: 'I've no need to do this job, you know, but I love every minute of it, save when I'm running late and then I want to know why! My job is to get people to their destinations on time, be they on business or pleasure.' George Lawrence died of a heart attack after a return working to London.

(Opposite)
The Sunday 4.5pm Wolverhampton-Euston nears Berkswell station on 15 June 1958 behind what was described as the 'black sheep of the family', No 45688 Polyphemus. *An ex-GWR corridor third is the second vehicle in the train.*
Michael Mensing

The Bushbury allocation of 'Jubilees' remained remarkably stable during the 1954-8 period. A total of nine 'Jubilees' at Bushbury was on the tight side, and during the mid-1950s their numbers fluctuated. As many as 11, for instance, were on strength in October 1957. As at 1 December 1956, the allocation at Bushbury comprised:

45555 *Quebec*	45734 *Meteor*
45647 *Sturdee*	45737 *Atlas*
45688 *Polyphemus*	45738 *Samson*
45709 *Implacable*	45741 *Leinster*
45733 *Novelty*	45742 *Connaught*

The same engines tended to predominate in everyday work, as well as in the logs of runs published in the railway press. The last series of engines, Nos 45733/4/7/8/41/2, seemed the best performers. Of these, No 45742 seems to have been something of a 'pet'. R. Brazier recalls: 'Great effort went into cleaning it every week. It came in on a Thursday and received all this attention to work the Saturday 9.45am Wolverhampton-Euston. Why it was so important to turn out No 45742 for this train, I don't know! I've been on better engines'. George Lawrence told George Green that No 45703 *Thunderer* was the best he had known on Bushbury's allocation but this engine departed for Crewe North shed in November 1954. From my own experience I remember that No 45688 appeared frequently, but George Green describes it as 'the black sheep of the family', and No 45555 as 'lovely to look at but perhaps not nice to know'.

What was it like to work a 'Jubilee' on the Wolverhampton-Euston turns? R. Brazier comments:

They could be temperamental. Some members of the class were diabolical! To get the best out of them, you had to work hard and put a lot of thought into the job. When leaving Bushbury shed, you needed to have a full tender tank and a full load of coal - you picked up water on Church Lawford, Castlethorpe and Bushey troughs. There was no difficulty in burning 7-7½ tons of coal each way on the London workings. Normally on the two-hour trains, it was a piece of cake - quite a decent turn. After a return trip to London, I usually went off to work on my allotment.

The competence of Bushbury's 'Jubilees' was of course no accident. The shed is remembered in the mid-1950s as a harmonious place under Shedmaster, Harry Austin. As elsewhere, there were members of the same family at the shed such as brothers R. and Ken Brazier with their father as one of the running foreman. Says J. Hurley: 'The team spirit was high, and the "Jubilees" were fussed over by Bill Acton, the Boilersmith. Everything was checked over when they came on shed. If, for instance, there were a couple of burnt firebars, Bill would have a cleaner in the firebox soon enough to replace them. At the 'X-Day' boiler washout, a doubtful brick arch would be re-bricked as new.' R. Brazier remembers: 'Faults booked by enginemen were rectified at Bushbury - if they had the parts they got on with the repair'.

With increasing traffic from the West Midlands during the late 1950s, heavier trains were inevitable. Early in 1958 it was said that the 6.45am from Wolverhampton often loaded to 12/13 bogies and was usually late into Euston if the 'Jubilee' was unassisted. As on the Midland Division of the LMR, there was recourse to expensive double-heading and the combination of a '7P' and a 'Black Five' was not exceptional on the two-hour Birmingham trains.

Time was running out by this stage for the 'Jubilees' in particular, and for steam generally at the southern end of the West Coast main line. Electrification work was in progress south of Crewe by the end of the decade and the winter 1958/9 timetable featured expanded schedules. This saw the demise of the two-hour trains, with 7-8 min being added to the timings of Euston-Wolverhampton trains, and no less than 16-20 min southbound.

These extended schedules were a prelude to a more dramatic development from 2 November 1959 when the majority of the Euston-Birmingham-Wolverhampton expresses were withdrawn, and in their place the service on the Western Region route to Birmingham was augmented. The effect was to reduce the remaining Euston-Birmingham-Wolverhampton trains to four each way, most of these being routed via Northampton.

The official justification for cutting-back the service was the impending reconstruction of Coventry station, and other modernisation works. Yet it coincided with the opening of the first lengthy stretch of the M1 motorway and the intro-

duction of the Midland Red motorway coaches linking London with Coventry and Birmingham.

The Bushbury 'Jubilees' had reached the end of their Top Link work. They and the shed's enginemen and other staff had served the railway well. For the greatly reduced Euston-Wolverhampton service that began on 2 November 1959, diagrams were introduced for '7Ps'. Bushbury received Nos 46122/41/3/53/8, the balance of workings on the service mostly passing to Crewe North '7Ps'. In the week ending 7 November 1959, Bushbury's 'Jubilees' Nos 45555, 45688, 45734/8/41/2 were transferred to Carlisle Upperby, the class ending its association with Bushbury in February 1960 once Nos 45647, 45709/37 had departed to join Aston's stud.

The shed's status declined in its remaining years, leading to closure at Easter 1965. That was when the Brazier brothers left the railway. They could have transferred to Stafford Road shed, Wolverhampton but knew that this shed, too, was due to close before long. Nowadays, the enginemen's houses have made way for Goodyear Tyres' premises, and the site of Bushbury shed is largely occupied by the Fordhouse Road industrial estate. Gala Clubs' bingo-hall has replaced the shed building.

3

A TALE OF BURNISHED BUFFERS
the Landore 'Castles'

On the Western Region, more attention has been given by writers to exceptional exploits by engines working on the Bristol and West of England roads, so it is Landore's turn to be in the limelight

Illusions are easily shattered, not least when it comes to past memories. I must admit that the Landore (Swansea) 'Castles' were chosen as a suitable subject primarily because I well remember the immaculate condition of these engines in the late 1950s, particularly Nos 5051, 5077, 5080 and 7028.

A casual glance at a selection of photographs of Landore 'Castles' in the early and mid-1950s soon revealed that many of them were far from immaculate... Much better were Can-

An immaculate Landore 'Castle' enters Newport in June 1957 when working the 2.30pm Neyland-Paddington.
George Heiron

Bruce Joyce and Alan Vickery at Landore shed in June 1994, in front of a former ex-Railway Operating Department tender which at one time ran with a GWR locomotive. The tender was used in a drain cleaning train, and has since been purchased for possible use.
Michael Harris

Study of the surviving management and Western Area Board records now in national archives soon dispelled any idea that the view from Paddington in the 1950s could be described as confident. Indeed, defeatist might not be too strong a word. The running of steam-hauled passenger trains on the Western Region of the time was anything but good. There were star turns such as the 'Bristolian', but experienced train recorder and locomotive fireman, Ken Phillips, makes a telling point when he says that the WR in steam days was like a symphony orchestra with a magnificent soloist, but otherwise very average players. Many of the trains were easily timed but unpunctual all the same.

The Great Western Railway invested heavily in South Wales. Although its pre-1914 hopes for transatlantic and Irish traffic routed through Fishguard were not fulfilled, there was enough business to provide full loads for the South Wales-Paddington expresses. These took advantage of the 'new' line through Badminton and, by Grouping, were hauled by the two-cylinder 'Saint' 4-6-0s. These capable engines were customary motive power for the six South Wales expresses booked to run the 133 miles from Paddington-Newport at an average speed of 57mph. Some of this class's best work was done on these trains until 'Stars' began to displace the 'Saints' from 1926, first at Cardiff Canton shed, then at Landore. The allocation of 'Castles' in any number to South Wales did not begin until the early 1930s. It was 1938 before the numbers of the class at Landore and Canton alike had reached double-figures.

At Nationalisation, Landore had 14 'Castles', including the preserved No 5051 which had first come to the shed in May 1936, and Nos 5013/6 which spent much of their working lives at the shed. From 1947, a number of brand-new 'Castles' were allocated to Landore, these being of the 7000 series with mechanical lubrication and boilers equipped with three-row superheaters. By May 1951, Landore's allocation comprised the following:

ton's well-polished 'Castles' and 'Halls'. However, most of the photographs were taken in the early or mid-1950s and enquiries soon provided an explanation for unkempt-looking engines from Landore.

The other illusion was perhaps not quite as fixed, because in my railway career I had something to do with the punctuality of trains. Whatever the writers on locomotive performance might have said, punctual running day-in, day-out was a different matter from an exceptional run when a recorder was on the footplate. On such occasions, a hand-picked engine was usually provided, and the enginemen were more conscious of the inspector's presence than of the man with a stop-watch on the fireman's side of the footplate!

4074 *Caldicot Castle*	7002 *Devizes Castle*
4078 *Pembroke Castle*	7003 *Elmley Castle*
4081 *Warwick Castle*	7009 *Athelney Castle*
4095 *Harlech Castle*	7012 *Barry Castle*
5002 *Ludlow Castle*	7018 *Drysllwyn Castle*
5013 *Abergavenny Castle*	7021 *Haverfordwest Castle*
5016 *Montgomery Castle*	7028 *Cadbury Castle*
5051 *Earl Bathurst*	
5072 *Hurricane*	
5093 *Upton Castle*	

Landore shed was opened in 1874, and replaced a depot at

Swansea High Street which dated from 1850. Landore shed was - and is - located within the triangle of running lines formed by the Cardiff-Swansea and former Swansea-West Wales main lines, with the connecting Landore West Curve (installed 1906) on the west side. The main shed of 1874 was stone-built, of four roads and 160ft long by 52ft wide. There was also a stone-built coaling stage.

Under the provisions of the Loans and Guarantees (1929) Act which aimed to relieve unemployment, the GWR built a new engine shed at Landore in 1932, adjacent to the exist-ing four-road building. The addition was known as the New Shed and, with four roads, was 210ft long by 67ft wide. At the same time the yard was remodelled. The coaling stage

The driver of Landore's well-cleaned 'Castle' No 5077 Fairey Battle climbs aboard at Cardiff General having done a spot of oiling round. This engine was a noted performer at Landore. The train is the 2.20pm Milford Haven-Paddington, the last up daytime South Wales express to the capital, and its engine was scheduled to return with the next day's down 'Pembroke Coast Express'. George Heiron

Landore engine and men: No 7009 Athelney Castle *sets out from Newport with the down 'Pembroke Coast Express' in this late 1950s' picture.*
George Heiron

was extended during 1944/5 to allow engines to be coaled from both sides, and at about this time a repair bay was built on to the side of the old shed and extended to incorporate the stores. Under the abortive coal-oil fuel conversion scheme of 1946-8, an installation was largely completed at Landore, and in its unfinished state was used for fuelling oil-burning engines.

Though Landore had an allocation of express locomotives, Neath was the major depot in the Neath Division and accordingly had more extensive repair facilities. To the GWR, Landore was coded LDR; its status vis-à-vis Neath was reflected in its post-1950 BR shed-code of 87E. The Landore 'Castles' also received attention at Danygraig shed, the former main works of the Rhondda and Swansea Bay Railway.

In 1938, Landore had an allocation of 57 engines, a total that altered little in succeeding years. Apart from the 'Castles', in later years Landore's fleet consisted mainly of mixed traffic types such as 'Halls', '56xx' 0-6-2Ts and '57xx' 0-6-0PTs. Also, there were '54/64xx' 0-6-0PTs for the Morriston branch and other auto-trains, as well as '42xx' and '72xx' eight-coupled tanks for banking and freight work.

The provision of fuelling facilities for dmus at High St was approved in 1957 and, as steam working declined, Landore was chosen as the site of a diesel locomotive maintenance and service depot. This entailed the demolition of most of the existing structures, and so the steam depot was closed in June 1961 for work to start, and its allocation of locomotives was dispersed. By May 1963, the new, diesel-only Landore was opened.

To return, however, to the early postwar days when Landore had its recently-built 'Castles'. Whatever the merits of the motive power, our railways were recovering all too slowly from the effects of the war. Performance was often dismally poor, not that the schedules of express trains were anything

A typical study of the steam age railway with plenty of wagonload traffic. The location is Pengam yards, to the east of Cardiff, and the date, July 1958. Worked by No 7028 Cadbury Castle, *the train is the up 'South Wales Pullman' - Landore engine and men, again.*
George Heiron

to write home about. When one of the railway journals reported with enthusiasm that on 2 January 1950 Landore 'Castle' No 7018 *Drysllwyn Castle* had arrived at Paddington six minutes early with the 14-coach 7.30am from Carmarthen, it sounded good. That was until the reader realised that the train had completed the 133-mile run from Newport in no less than 162 minutes, at an average speed of 49mph or so. At the time, such running probably *was* good. Few other schedules of the principal up South Wales trains of that time were better.

For a portrait of the Landore of those days, I am indebted to Alan Vickery and Bruce Joyce. Both began work at Landore in 1941 and progressed through driving and firing at this, and other sheds, to become traction inspectors. Both

retired from the railway service during the 1980s. They remember the immediate postwar years as the 'bad old days'. The coal was of poor quality, an appreciable minority of those on the railway lacked any interest in the job, and, when working the 'double-home' (lodging turns) to London, they remember the overnight accommodation as unspeakably bad.

From the latter part of World War 2, most of the Top Link passenger workings to/from London constituted 'double-home' turns, performed by Landore engines and men. Previously, Landore engines seem to have been remanned at Cardiff, or Swindon. The enginemen at Cardiff Canton were able to complete a return trip to London within an 8hr span, but this was not possible from Swansea, for the single journey took some $4\frac{1}{2}$-5 hours in the early postwar years. For every 15 miles over 140 miles on these turns, the men received 1 hour's pay, so that a single trip to London paid the same as a 12-hour day.

Alan and Bruce remember that there was no difficulty finding a fireman prepared to work to London. Usual expe-

Landore's No 7012 Barry Castle *takes water from Goring troughs on 12 August 1956, at the head of the 3.55am Fishguard Harbour-Paddington. This train ran via Felin Fran and the Swansea Avoiding Line.*

Some drivers disliked taking water on the troughs, and for the fireman it was a matter of careful judgment and hard work to wind-up the scoop in time, particularly if the engine was ex-works and the apparatus stiff.

D. M. C. Hepburne-Scott/Rail Archive Stephenson

(Opposite – top)
Landore's No 5051 Earl Bathurst *makes a fine sight on 9 October 1955 as it heads a lengthy parcels train along the down relief line towards Didcot. Possibly this was a running-in turn for an ex-works engine - No 5051 had just emerged from overhaul at Swindon, and was doubtless returning home. By then it had run not far short of one million miles.*

The engine arrived at Landore on 24 May 1936 and remained at the same depot until transfer to Neath on 23 June 1961. Alan Vickery remembers cleaning No 5051, shortly after he joined the GWR in 1941.

D. M. C. Hepburne-Scott/Rail Archive Stephenson

rience was that an engine crew would work to London and back once in a week, more rarely, twice-weekly. They recall: 'They would still pay you if the locomotive failed, but not if the journey was terminated by an "Act of God". You were paid if the train was cancelled, but received a 'mileage' payment if there was a diversion, say, via Bath and the Berks & Hants. Some of those diversions could seem endless'.

Their opinion is that considerable skill and hard work were attached to these Top Link jobs. Sometimes, a good fireman might get off his engine reasonably clean, but that was sel-

(Opposite – lower)
Landore's No 5051 Earl Bathurst *makes a pleasing sight as it stands at Old Oak Common on 21 September 1958, in-between trains when on a double-home working. Note the scoured buffers and chimney cap, and polished safety valve bonnet. No 5051 had last received major attention at Swindon Works in October 1957.*

R. C. Riley

dom the case during the late 1940s/early 1950s. There were plenty of 'rough trips' and coal was usually to blame, particularly the much-hated ovoids that at the time were so often a feature of Western Region operations. Alan remembers his first trip to London on a double-home working with Landore's No 5013 *Abergavenny Castle*. 'It wasn't very good. We had struggled up to Badminton with half-a-pot of water and 180 lbs of steam. To my amazement, my driver, H. Humphries, was singing an operatic aria at the top of his voice, breaking off to say, "On form, today, boy, this is a great trip - usually we have just 140 lbs on the clock!"' The 'Castles' were set to blow off at 225 lbs.

The established pattern began to change from late 1952 when five, new 'Britannias' were allocated to Canton although none of the Landore turns on the London trains was affected. With the summer 1953 timetable, a new pair of expresses were introduced with the proud title of the 'Pembroke Coast Express': the 10.55am Paddington-Pembroke Dock and 1pm return. Also, the 11.55am from Paddington was accelerated by no less than 23min overall, giving some indication of the slackness of the previous schedule.

It was true, of course, that fast running was not really possible west of Cardiff and that there were pathing problems, given the flows of freight trains, and the resultant chance of delays through the Severn Tunnel. Up expresses faced a staged climb of nearly 20 miles from the depths of the Tunnel to beyond Badminton, comprising six miles at 1 in 100, the rest at 1 in 300.

Landore's No 7021 Haverfordwest Castle *works the down 'Capitals United Express', passing Old Oak Common East box on 29 August 1959. Its train consists of at least 12 BR Standard coaches, mostly in chocolate and cream livery. The weight of trains such as the 'CUE' was one reason for the slow schedules of most of the South Wales expresses. For the summers of 1958/9, this express was worked turn and turn about by Old Oak and Landore 'Castles' instead of the Canton 'Britannias' usually associated with this train at the time.*

When photographed, the engine was becoming due for works attention and it went to Swindon for a heavy general overhaul that November.
R. C. Riley

At first sight, these gradients do not appear taxing but the cumulative effects of the passage of the Severn Tunnel, succeeded by the single-bore Patchway Tunnel, so often full of smoke from a preceding train, and the climb to Badminton were easily underestimated by the casual observer. As Alan and Bruce recall: 'You were at it pretty well all the time as a fireman on an up express - firing all the time from the Tunnel to Badminton, and again from Swindon to Didcot. On the down run, you were firing continuously between Paddington and Badminton, and had to fire like hell from Newport to Cardiff. You only sat down between Badminton and the Tunnel.'

David Tomkiss remembers overhearing a Landore fireman responding to an enquiry about his worst nightmare on the London run. 'Not enough water at Cardiff or Newport to fill the tank, and having to take water on Undy troughs, dirty water that. Brought to a stand at Severn Tunnel West, then checked at Cattybrook. Patchway Tunnel full of smoke, a boiler full of froth on the climb to Badminton, and a couple more checks before Wootton Bassett. By then, you'd have had the heart knocked out of you - and so would the fire.'

It was often hard work, and during the early 1950s the Western Region's record for the punctuality of its passenger trains was poor. Special attention was given to the running of certain trains, such as the 6.30am Swansea-Paddington and the 3.55pm Paddington-Fishguard Harbour. Every day, the running superintendents concerned with these trains had to wire Gilbert Matthews, Superintendent of the Line, with details of their performance, according to the minutes of a WR superintendents' meeting held in January 1952. Locomotives and bad coal were to blame, according to the railway managers.

In October 1953, the WR's mechanical and electrical engineer, R. A. Smeddle informed the operators that certain 'Kings' and 'Castles' had been 'modified to give improved performance... (there is) a possibility of accelerating trains on main routes. The loads being stipulated represent the

maximum - there is no margin for additional coaches.' The modifications resulted from experimental work by Sam Ell at Swindon which evolved improved draughting for the 'Kings' and 'Castles', and from 1953 onwards this was applied to a number of engines. From the same year, new 'Castle' boilers were built with four-row superheaters, the view being that a higher degree of superheat was desirable.

Early in 1954, the accelerated timings were finalised, for introduction from the summer service. Such speeded-up trains depended on the availability of specially selected 'Castles' and, in Landore's case, these worked the 'Pembroke Coast Express' in each direction. A penalty was paid as the accelerated 'Special Load' timings limited a 'Castle' to a maximum of 315 tons although the load of the named train

Working an up West Wales-Paddington express of the late 1950s, No 5041 Tiverton Castle *approaches Badminton station, the summit of the climb from the depths of the Severn Tunnel. No 5041 had been transferred from Newton Abbot in 1955, and while at Landore was considered a 'good 'un' and regularly used for the most demanding workings.*
George Heiron

was usually eight coaches. Apart from the revitalised 'Castles', other improvements were apparent. At Landore, Oakdale coal was made available for the top-link engines. 'It was a different story with steaming, then', comments Bruce Joyce, 'the steam gauge was on the needle all the time and it was a pleasure to work on the engine'. In place of the noisome 'digs' at 3/6 a night, a new hostel at Old Oak Common was available to the enginemen rostered on the double home turns.

With the new timings, the down 'Pembroke Coast Express' was faster by 11 minutes to Cardiff, but the up working had been accelerated by no less than half-an-hour throughout from Pembroke Dock to Paddington. This was still a wearisome business for the passenger and the journey occupied just over $6\frac{1}{2}$ hours, during which there were two changes of engine necessitated by the train's two reversals, at Carmarthen and Swansea.

The Landore 'Castles' must have passed muster on the faster timings for, in the summer 1955 service, the down

'Pembroke Coast Express' was promoted to a better than mile-a-minute run from Paddington to Newport. In 128 minutes, this journey was faster by nine minutes than any previous timing. Overall, the train now took 25min less to reach Pembroke Dock. The schedule to Newport was later eased, but the time recovered on the section to Cardiff; there had been a tight margin into Newport behind an express from Birmingham, with the result that the driver of the 'Pembroke Coast Express' risked being brought to a stand at East Usk Jct. The summer 1955 timetable also saw the introduction of the 'South Wales Pullman', down at 9.55am (changed to 8.50am from 1957) from Paddington, and back at 4.35 pm from Swansea. Both workings were covered by a Landore engine and men. Although limited to eight Pullman cars, equal to 320 tons, the new service did not feature the fast timings of the 'Pembroke Coast Express'.

What about locomotive performance, as measured by recorders on the footplate, or from the train? Soon after the June 1955 accelerations, O. S. Nock travelled on Landore's

Another transfer from the West Country to Landore was No 4099
Kilgerran Castle *which came from Penzance shed in late 1957.*
With the fireman at work, No 4099 takes the up 'South Wales
Pullman' past Wapley sidings, Westerleigh in this late 1950s' study.
It looks as though one of the Pullman brake cars has been marked
'off tick', and replaced by a BR Standard brake composite.
George Heiron

No 7009 *Athelney Castle*, loaded to eight coaches with the down 'Pembroke Coast Express'. The Landore enginemen were Driver Jack 'Electric' Jenkins and Fireman Alec Northway. Nock described 'Electric' as: 'an artist indeed in the handling of his engine' and he lived up to his name so far as running was concerned; there was time in hand throughout. Between Paddington and Newport the engine was worked economically enough to average 27 gallons/mile water consumption. On down workings such as this, water was normally taken from the troughs at Chipping Sodbury and Magor.

'Electric' was a stickler when it came to his engine's turnout. The buffers were silvered at Landore before departure and he asked for - and got, mind you - a new set of headlamps for every double-home turn, making sure they were were hidden while his 'Castle' stabled at Old Oak Common overnight. Alan and Bruce remember 'Electric' Jenkins well: 'He was a hard runner and had to be right-time at Paddington. On the footplate, he was never still, always busy. He

spent the journey hanging on the whistle-chain - whistling at the signals if they were against him.'

Ken Phillips recorded five runs on the down 'Pembroke Coast Express' in the 1955-7 period. The engines he timed were Landore's Nos 5013 *Abergavenny Castle*, 5074 *Hampden* (then recently transferred to the shed) and 7009 *Athelney Castle*, as well as an interloper in the shape of Old Oak's No 5055 *Earl of Eldon*. Against the 128-minute timing to Newport, only one run showed that there was much in hand, even with just 265/275 tons gross. On the gently rising stretch from Didcot to Swindon the 'Castles' were running at 65-72 mph, depending on the load, while on only two runs were downhill maxima of 80 mph recorded. On a timing of 145 min from Newport to Paddington a 'Castle' on the eight-coach up 'Pembroke Coast Express' was not really extended, but there was an enterprising run with Landore's No 4078 *Pembroke Castle* 'overloaded' to 355 tons gross. The Landore crew, Driver Tom Talbot and Fireman Ron Gabriel, left Swansea 8min late and reached Paddington 5min early; even with this load, their running showed that, unchecked, a time of $127^3/_4$ min could have been achieved between Newport and Paddington.

The Western Region could have achieved consistently better results if there had been a concerted effort to rectify the reasons for unpunctual operation. The management of the time was all too ready to find excuses. Yet the standard of punctuality of the Region's Class '1' trains was, to quote the minutes of the Western Area Board meeting of March 1957, 'inferior to the standards of other Regions.'

And the excuses? That there were mechanical defects on locomotives, poor quality coal and 'difficulty in obtaining the right type of engine for the job owing to arrears of maintenance.' Chairman Reginald Hanks's contribution to the debate was to suggest that 'drivers were notching-up too soon, thus retarding acceleration.' The litany of excuses went on: former GWR engines were having to burn coal of lower calorific value than they were accustomed to; the South Wales service was dogged by late-running freight trains and maintenance work in the Severn Tunnel, and, inevitably, Board members 'enquired whether delays might not also be attributable to the use of "Britannia" class engines stationed at Cardiff'. Heads should have rolled at this craven abrogation of responsibility - and would have done on some other Regions!

Out of this Board discussion came one definite decision, that the Eastern Region practice of a removable plate bearing the names of the engine crew should be fixed to the cabside as 'this might have some psychological effect upon men in performance of their duties'. It was a poor reflection of the management's view of their enginemen and motive power, and many drivers responded by leaving the cabside plates in their lockers.

More effective measures were employed locally. At Landore, the arrival of Roy White as Shedmaster had the effect of tidying up Landore and it was his initiative that produced the shining 'Castles' with their scoured and polished buffers, chimney caps and safety valve bonnets that I so well remember in the late 1950s and early 1960s.

The Top Link workings on the South Wales route were shared between Landore and Old Oak Common, both sheds using 'Castles', and Canton, with its 'Britannias'. Old Oak engines and men generally worked as far west only as Cardiff. During the mid-1950s there had been some dispute between the men at Old Oak Common shed and management, with the result that this depot had lost most of its double-home workings to/from Swansea. To maintain the depot's route knowledge, its No 2 Link retained a duty with the 6.55pm Paddington-Fishguard Harbour, worked to Swansea with an Old Oak 'Castle'. Engine and men returned the following day from Swansea with the 11.10am Milford Haven-Paddington. Another Old Oak engine and men turn covered the 8.55pm FO Paddington-Milford Haven, and the next day's up 'Pembroke Coast Express. Swindon and Carmarthen engines also covered a couple of workings on the South Wales main line.

A Landore 'Castle' alternated with one from Old Oak shed on the diagram covering the 4.35pm Neyland-Paddington parcels, to return with the 9.25pm passenger to Cardiff via Gloucester. During the summer of 1958, a Landore and Old Oak Common 'Castle' alternated with the working of the down 'Capitals United Express' which before long reverted to haulage by a Canton 'Britannia'. Also of significance was Landore's turn with the 8.30pm Whitland-Kensington milk train, worked as far as Cardiff. Routed via Felin Fran, on this train a 'Castle' could be loaded to a maximum of 18 milk-tankers, equal to 505 tons; in Alan and Bruce's view, this was one of the hardest workings as the tank wagons pulled more heavily than passenger coaches. Landore 'Castles' had other turns, west of Swansea and, in earlier years, to Birmingham and back (remanned at Cardiff) and to and from Banbury via Swindon and Oxford on the summer Swansea-York/Newcastle and return train.

By 1959/60, the double-home duties to London worked by the Landore 'Castles' looked like this:

2.30pm Swansea-Paddington Day 'A', standby at Old Oak for the other Landore engines, then the 11.55am Paddington-Swansea Day 'B'

3.45pm Swansea-Paddington (the 'Pembroke Coast Express') Day 'A', returning with the 8.55am ex-Paddington Day 'B'

4.30pm Swansea-Paddington (the 'South Wales Pullman') Day 'A', returning with the down 'Pullman', the 8.50am ex-Paddington, Day 'B'

5.30pm Swansea-Paddington, Day 'A', returning with the 10.55am (the 'Pembroke Coast Express') ex-Paddington, Day 'B'

Landore's allocation of 'Castles' in April 1960 comprised:

4074* *Caldicot Castle*	5039 *Rhuddlan Castle*
4076 *Carmarthen Castle*	5041 *Tiverton Castle*
4093* *Dunster Castle*	5051 *Earl Bathurst*
4094 *Dynevor Castle*	5077 *Fairy Battle*
4097* *Kenilworth Castle*	5091 *Cleeve Castle*
4099 *Kilgerran Castle*	7009 *Athelney Castle*
5004 *Llanstephan Castle*	7021 *Haverfordwest Castle*
5013 *Abergavenny Castle*	7028 *Cadbury Castle*
5016 *Montgomery Castle*	

Those engines with double blastpipes and chimneys are denoted by asterisks. There had been a major reallocation of 'Castles' during the mid-1950s which brought No 4099 to Landore from Penzance in exchange for 4095, No 4076 from Chester in place of 4078, and other newcomers Nos 5041 and 5077, the latter having displaced No 7018. Most of the allocation were well-regarded, with the exception of No 4097, castigated for being 'very weak'.

Based on the available mileage figures from the engine record cards, during the 1950s and until the depot's closure, the Top Link Landore 'Castles' clocked up an annual total of 40,000-50,000 miles. Comparison might be made, although the conditions were very different, with the 70,000 annual mileage recorded during this period for some of the 'Britannias' allocated to Norwich. At the time, the average daily mileage of a 'Castle', including days stopped for boiler washouts and repairs, was some 150 miles. As a guide to serviceability, the 'top' 'Castles' were running 90,000 miles between general repairs. Among the best performers at Landore on all counts were Nos 5041, 5077, 7009 and 7028.

The Landore 'Castles' continued to work on the Paddington-South Wales expresses until the closure of their depot to steam and their transfer elsewhere, with effect from 13 June 1961. Nos 4090/3/9, 5004/13/41/4/51/62/74/8 went to 87A, Neath and Nos 4076/8/81/94, 5006/16/77/80/91, 7021/8 to 87F, Llanelly. At their new depots they were smartly turned out and continued to work on the South Wales expresses until, beginning in March 1962, these were dieselised using Hymek diesel-hydraulics. The diesel Blue Pullmans had been introduced between Paddington and Swansea in September 1961. For a little while longer the displaced 'Castles' were to be seen on other Class '1' trains east or, more usually, west of Swansea. Some went to store for a time, as was the case with Nos 5080 and 7028, but their time was running out, and all had gone by 1965. Landore depot has survived into the privatised present and is used by Great Western Trains.

4

RESPECTED, BUT NOT LOVED

'A1' Pacifics at Gateshead and Heaton sheds

More has appeared in print on the Kings Cross Pacifics than about those allocated to northern sheds. The Tyneside depots are overdue for attention, particularly the engines and men that worked Gateshead's Lodge Link.

I f all goes well, it should one day be possible to travel behind an 'A1' in the shape of No 60163 *Tornado*, thanks to the endeavours of the A1 Steam Locomotive Trust. But whether there will be the chance of a Kings Cross to Newcastle trip is another matter. Nowadays, with electric traction, the 268 miles between Thames and Tyne is no more than a journey of $2^3/_4$hr, whereas the steam-hauled 'Talisman' of 1958 took $4^1/_2$hr, and the crew working a sleeping car express faced five hours' hard graft on the footplate. Although by that time there were eight through engine workings between Kings Cross and Newcastle and vice versa, other East Coast expresses continued to change engines at intermediate points.

(Previous page)
For some time during the 1950s, Gateshead shed had the honour of working the up 'Flying Scotsman' from Edinburgh to Newcastle. Away from Edinburgh Waverley on 23 September 1955 comes No 60155 Borderer, an engine frequently used on the London lodging turn, but here duly carrying the headboard for the 'Scotsman' whose first vehicle is one of the few LNER postwar full brakes painted not in all-over carmine, but in carmine and cream.
D. M. C. Hepburne-Scott/Rail Archive Stephenson

(Above)
The 'A1s' changed their appearance during the 1950s. In this 24 March 1951 photograph, No 60147 of Gateshead still lacks its name and also retains a rimmed chimney. In fact, it was the last of the class to be named: this took place in March 1952.
The engine is working the 2.35pm stopping train to Peterborough out of Grantham and the occupants of the elderly Hull & Barnsley and North Eastern coaches in tow might be facing a lively ride! No 60147 is on what might seem to be a running-in turn, but at this stage it was midway between calls to Doncaster for Intermediate Heavy repairs, the next visit being in July 1951.
T. G. Hepburn/Rail Archive Stephenson

The 49 'A1s' went into traffic during the first 18 months of Nationalisation, turned out from Doncaster and Darlington Works. The majority carried the LNER green livery (with British Railways lettering) which looked so startling -

when clean - in those drab early postwar surroundings. They were imposing - and *new*, for, in common with those entering service in southern England, these Pacifics had not endured the war years that debilitated much of the locomotive stock. But if the 'A1s' entering service at sheds along the East Coast main line were new, and of the latest design, why could they not work throughout from London to Tyneside?

Through London-Newcastle workings by LNER Pacifics had featured in prewar days when there were the London-Edinburgh runs of the 'Coronation', and the summer non-stop 'Flying Scotsman'. In the mid/late 1930s, there were usually four Kings Cross-Newcastle workings each way on weekdays, including the 'Silver Jubilee'. Until 1938, a Pacific made just one such trip in 24hr, its crew lodging away from home alternate days. In a bid to improve utilisation, in-between the Newcastle trips it was decided to fit in a round trip from Kings Cross to Peterborough (or Grantham) and back. Additional, more complicated diagrams were introduced for Kings Cross and Gateshead 'A4' Pacifics in March 1939. For Gateshead shed, one of its engines was worked by eight sets of men from four depots during a turn which took the 'A4' from Newcastle to Edinburgh and London before the return home. Wartime workings were very different and followed abandonment of the arduous through runs whose successful operation had demanded high standards of maintenance and enginemanship.

(*Top*)

Despite its status, Gateshead shed was not well-equipped to handle large engines, the Pacifics were dealt with in the cramped, three-road Pacific shed fashioned in the 1920s from the tender shop of Gateshead Works. It was not until the 1950s that the shed received a 70ft turntable: until then, the Pacifics had to use the triangle nearby.

No 60143, still un-named and in LNER-style green livery, attracts attention from enginemen and a member of the shed staff at its home shed on 25 June 1950.

H. C. Casserley

(*Above*)

Gateshead's No 60124 Kenilworth was to be one of the final survivors of the class but is seen here at Grantham on 4 October 1952, by now with lipped chimney and in Brunswick green livery. It has given way to another engine on an up express and is heading for servicing on Grantham shed.

John P. Wilson/Rail Archive Stephenson

From the summer of 1947, longer workings began to reappear, with Tyneside Pacifics coming up to London with a break of turn at Grantham. The next year, there was a solitary Heaton Pacific diagram on an up daytime express, returning with the down 'Night Scotsman' to Newcastle. The same depot worked the 'Tees-Tyne Pullman' each way for this train's first year of operation, and for this the new 'A1s' made their debut, No 60116 being put to work along with Nos 60126/7. Names were applied to these engines in due course.

Kings Cross took over the working of the 'Tees-Tyne Pullman' from the next summer as a lodging turn. While this form of working was always welcome to crews in terms of pay, it was far from attractive in the days when the standard of overnight accommodation was little short of appalling. In 1945, the railway trades unions had begun negotiations for the abolition of lodging turns. These had been greatly reduced in number by 1949 when the Railway Executive changed tack and proposed their reintroduction. That May, enginemen at Gateshead, Heaton and York refused to work the new timetables and took unofficial strike action.

One of the stars of the Gateshead 'A1s' was No 60155 Borderer which with No 60154 featured on the shed's lodging turn with sleeping car expresses. On 9 May 1954, No 60155, neither really dirty nor what could be called clean, poses on Top Shed (Kings Cross) alongside 'V2' No 60903 and Kings Cross 'A4' No 60034 Lord Faringdon.
No 60155's previous general overhaul at Doncaster was completed in October 1953, and it next went for a 'general' in January 1955, having completed nearly 110,000 miles without an intervening unscheduled works' visit.
Brian Morrison

Gradually, resistance on Tyneside to lodging turns declined but already Kings Cross-Newcastle lodge turns had passed to Kings Cross shed. York men's opposition to lodging turns was such that their shed lost its chance to participate in the working of expresses with Kings Cross and Haymarket, a plan which if implemented would have reduced the status of Gateshead. Before long, there were enough volunteers at Gateshead to make it possible to roster three sets of men for the shed's principal turn southwards on the 10.20pm Edinburgh-Kings Cross, to return with the down 'Night Scotsman'. Each crew worked for a fortnight on the night trains, and then spent a week on shed duties. This was to become Gateshead's classic working with 'A1s', on which engines and men set up a first-class record for consistency and reliability, most particularly with Nos 60154/5, of which more later.

If, in 1949, the opposition of some enginemen to lodging turns had made it difficult to introduce long-distance engine workings on the East Coast route south of Newcastle, for the summer 1950 timetable the authorities felt confident in effecting a clean sweep of existing practices. Workings for engines and men were radically changed, with the aim of making the maximum use of both resources at Kings Cross, Gateshead and Heaton sheds. Engine changing on expresses was almost eliminated at Grantham and Peterborough, and greatly reduced at York.

The initial impression was that the Tyneside sheds were working almost everything. Heaton engines - 'A1s', 'A2s' and 'A3s' - worked three up expresses to London, and returned the same evening, including haulage of the crack 5.35pm down. Gateshead Pacifics came up to town on three expresses including the Edinburgh sleeper, the 'Flying Scotsman' and the afternoon Scotsman - all premier workings, to return with the down 'Night Scotsman', the New-

castle sleeper and the next day's morning Kings Cross-Glasgow express.

Some changes were made in the winter 1950/51 timetable, but the overall results of the altered pattern of engine working were little short of disastrous. Even with the slow schedules of the time, timekeeping was very poor and there were numerous locomotive failures and substitutions. An all-out effort was made to counter the difficulties, with an extensive use of inspectors to monitor working on the footplate, but in the postwar environment of deferred renewals, poor working conditions and doubtful coal the resources were simply unable to deliver the goods.

Gateshead 'A1s' nonetheless put up some fine performances, highlighted in early 1951 by No 60147 *North Eastern* which, after three consecutive runs on the up 'Flying Scotsman', in each case returning home the same night, on the fourth day was borrowed by Kings Cross to work to Leeds and back, before returning home that evening with the 8.20pm to Edinburgh. The Pacific completed 1,720 miles in

Gateshead and Heaton engines were often borrowed by Kings Cross to cover its varied turns and this seems to be the case with No 60151 Midlothian *which on 20 September 1958 was heading the 12.45pm Cambridge-Kings Cross slow train near Brookmans Park.*
K. L. Cook/Rail Archive Stephenson

under 100 hours.

With the winter 1951/2 timetable, all through Kings Cross-Newcastle workings were discontinued, with the exception of Kings Cross's lodging turn that covered the 'Tees-Tyne Pullman' in both directions, and Gateshead's by now well-established lodging turn covering the 'Night Scotsman' each way.

It is now time to turn to the engines at work from Gateshead and Heaton depots, the deliveries of 'A1s' to both sheds being as shown in Table 1.

Nos 60114-29/53-62 were built at Doncaster Works, and the remainder (60130-52) by Darlington. Although the earlier engines were outshopped in LNER-style green paintwork, Nos 60127-9/53-62 were finished in the short-lived BR blue livery with BR 'cycling-lion' on the tender-sides. At first, they carried the severe chimney with rim, later replaced by the attractive lipped pattern. Another feature of their entry into service is that they ran unnamed until 1950-2, one of the last to be dealt with being Gateshead's No 60147. Given their normal sphere of operation, the names and asso-

ciations were particularly appropriate. Nos 60154/5 were from the batch of five engines equipped with roller bearings on all axles.

The 'A1s' were eagerly accepted for use on the heavy express passenger trains of the East Coast route, so characteristic of the early postwar years. Details of mileages run in their first years of service are available from the surviving engine record cards, and a sample is worthy of inclusion:

Gateshead	60124	106,000 from new to July 1950, and general overhaul at Doncaster
Gateshead	60142	101,000 from new to September 1950, and general overhaul at Doncaster
Heaton	60116	100,000 from new to January 1950, and general overhaul at Doncaster

(Opposite)
In this atmospheric
photograph of Bill
Anderson's, you can almost
hear the characteristic sound
of an 'A1' as, on an August
evening in 1958, Heaton's No
60127 Wilson Worsdell
hustles past Innerwick, on the
descent from Grantshouse.
The engine is on the shed's
prestige duty with the down
'Queen of Scots' and,
assuming all was well, it would
have worked south earlier in
the day with the up Pullman,
and before long would return
to Newcastle with an up
sleeping car express.
W. J. Verden Anderson/
Rail Archive Stephenson

TABLE 1

Engine No.	Name*	To depot
Gateshead engines		
60115	Meg Merrilies	New, 3 September 1948
60124	Kenilworth	New, 23 March 1949
60129	Guy Mannering	4 September 1949, ex-York (new, 15 June 1949)
60132	Marmion	New, 18 October 1948
60135	Madge Widfire	New, 18 November 1948
60137	Redgauntlet	New, 3 December 1948
60142	Edward Fletcher	New, 2 February 1949
60143	Sir Walter Scott	New, 22 February 1949
60145	Saint Mungo	New, 23 March 1949
60147	North Eastern	New, 13 April 1949
60150	Willbrook	10 July 1949, ex-Heaton
60151	Midlothian	New, 30 June 1949
60154	Bon Accord	New, 23 September 1949
60155	Borderer	New, 29 September 1949
Heaton engines		
60116	Hal o' the Wynd	New, 8 October 1948
60126	Sir Vincent Raven	New, 27 April 1949
60127	Wilson Worsdell	New, 13 May 1949
60150	Willbrook	New, 15 June 1949, to Gateshead, 10 July 1949

TABLE 2

Engine	Details	Date to Doncaster	Mileage between heavy overhauls
60154	New	September 1949	
	Intermediate/Heavy Repair (boiler change*)	March 1951	(128,868)
	General*	July 1952	251,743
	General*	November 1953	129,339
	General*	November 1955	121,766
	General*	March 1957	104,006
	General*	August 1958	120,524
	Transferred to York shed		
	General*	March 1960	112,804
	General	September 1962	103,000

Transferred to Neville Hill July 1963, condemned at depot, 4 October 1965

Engine	Details	Date to Doncaster	Mileage between heavy overhauls
60155	New	September 1949	
	Intermediate/Heavy Repair (boiler change*)	January 1951	(121,272)
	General*	April 1952	237,050
	General*	August 1953	121,346
	General*	January 1955	109,924
	General*	May 1956	102,919
	General*	February 1958	141,846
	General*	September 1959	138,197
	General*	June 1961	104,000

Transferred to Tweedmouth, September 1962; to York November 1962. Withdrawn 4 October 1965

The various stopping trains between Edinburgh, Berwick and Newcastle were notoriously uneconomic, but at least there is some post or parcels traffic in this up Class 'A' train, entering Dunbar, c 1959. The engine is Gateshead's No 60115 Meg Merrilies.
T. G. Hepburn/Rail Archive Stephenson

These were above-average figures for the class which as a whole attained an average of some 93,000 miles between heavy repairs, taking 1953 as an example. As an indication of work performed, the mileage figures quoted indicate an average of 5,900-7,700 miles per month. This was admirable although in later years some Kings Cross 'A4s' were recorded as completing over 9,000 miles in a four-week period.

The accompanying Table 2 shows abbreviated repair life histories for Nos 60154/5 which must come near to being regarded as not only the most successful postwar LNER design Pacifics, but giving the best value of any of the postwar British Pacifics. No doubt they were in Mr J. F. Harrison's mind when in 1961 he delivered his Presidential Address to the Institution of Locomotive Engineers. He described the five roller bearing equipped 'A1s' as: 'intended to give a better performance than any previous Pacific, to be cheaper to maintain, and to run increased mileages per annum and between general repairs'. He noted that one of the five had completed 1 million miles since new - No 60155 was possibly the engine - this figure representing 228 miles run for every calendar day since outshopping from Doncaster. In fact, the average daily mileage of the class as a whole was 202, as against an average of all BR express passenger engines of 170.

Much of Britain's industrial output of the early postwar years suffered from poor manufacturing standards, and some of the 'A1s' were not immune. In addition, the chassis design was their Achilles' heel. Various observers commented on the engines' bad riding, claiming that they appeared to pivot on a vertical axis passing through the centre driving axle. Some 'A1s' developed no more than a nosing action at 40-50mph, but others would lurch sideways unexpectedly and could prove unbearably uncomfortable at over 60mph.

Whether cause or effect, some engines suffered from fractures of the middle cylinders, or from defective castings, at least in early days. Sample failures include: 60126, June 1950; 60132, November 1950; 60135, left-hand cylinder loose, July 1949, right-hand cylinder flange cracked, problems with the centre cylinder and the left-hand cylinder working loose, May 1950-August 1951; 60137, centre cylinder fracture, April 1950, left-hand cylinder casting fractured, May 1951. Nos 60143/7 were also stopped for similar problems. The flanges by which the cylinders were bolted to the frames were not strong enough, and were later made thicker. In time, stiffening plates were welded and riveted to the frames between the inside cylinder and the rear of the motion stay. The class as a whole retained a reputation for rough riding.

Nos 60154/5 worked almost regularly on Gateshead's lodging turn during the early 1950s, and until the summer of 1954. Although the schedules of the 'Night Scotsman' were at first sight undemanding, requiring an average speed of no more than 45 mph on the non-stop Newcastle-Kings Cross run, in both directions in the winter timetable the trains were booked to load to 14 vehicles, equal to 484 tons tare. That meant hard work on the climb to Stoke in both directions, out of London to Potters Bar, and to Stevenage

Grubby and far from steam-tight, on 6 January 1960 Heaton's No 60126 Sir Vincent Raven *begins the shed's diagram which involves haulage of the up 'Northumbrian' from Newcastle to Peterborough, after which it will return north to York with the Colchester-Glasgow, a passenger and parcels train.*

The engine is being put to it on the 1 in 120/101 climb from Durham to Relly Mill. Dimly visible in No 60126's train is one of the Gresley articulated restaurant car triplets used on this service until 1961.

Ian S. Carr

on the up run. Added to this was the likelihood of signal checks from the heavy nighttime freight traffic of the period, and so engines and men faced an onerous task. In their absence, Gateshead relied on its 'A4s', Nos 60005/16 being used early in March 1956, for instance.

Former Driver Andy Robson spent over six years in the Gateshead Lodge Link, as fireman to Jack Ridley. Commencing in May 1950, Andy reckons that he completed 335,368 miles as fireman in the link, and for 95% of the time worked on Nos 60154/5. The Lodge Link comprised three regular sets of men, all volunteers: Drivers Jack Ridley, Ralph Silson and Harry Lazenby, and Firemen Andy Robson, Tommy Turner and Ozzy Anderson, the last-named being replaced by Jonah Barrett for the last two years of the link. There were four sets of spare men.

Andy Robson remembers that the week started by signing on at 11.45pm on a Sunday night, to work the 1.1am up 'Night Scotsman' to Kings Cross. The 'A1' was then booked to be on Kings Cross shed until it was ready to work the down 'Night Scotsman' but from time to time it was used for a fill-in turn to Peterborough and back. In such cases, there were consequences for the rest of the week's work, as Andy

Robson explains:

> Water-softening was the rule in the GN area. If our engine
> had been borrowed by Kings Cross, usually the 'A1' would
> be priming as a result of the treated water when working the
> down 'Night Scotsman' on Monday night. It was booked to
> work the 'North Briton' to Edinburgh and back on the Tues-
> day, and be ready for that night's Kings Cross working. But
> if there had been a bad bout of priming the engine was
> stopped at Gateshead for a boiler washout, and so missed its
> return trip to Edinburgh. Locomotives might work from
> Newcastle to Edinburgh and back for a fortnight or more,
> and in the absence of the treated water did not need anything
> like as much washing out.

Gateshead Pacifics worked as far as Peterborough in the
course of three other diagrams. Taking 1955 as an example,
one worked in on the Glasgow-Colchester overnight train,
to return with the 10.5am Kings Cross-Glasgow; another
brought in the 8am Newcastle-Kings Cross, heading north
with the 'Heart of Midlothian'; and the third arrived with
the celebrated Newcastle Delaval-Hornsey stock train, to
depart during the small hours with the 12.55am Kings
Cross-Edinburgh sleeping car train. By this time, Heaton no

Carrying a Tweedmouth shed-plate, No 60127 Wilson Worsdell
*smokes its way past Manors on 1 August 1964 with a relief express
for Edinburgh Waverley. Its train is composed of postwar LNER
design coaches, one or two Gresley teak-bodied vehicles and BR
Standards. No 60127 is carrying a Diagram 117 boiler with a
round dome carried further forward on the barrel.*
Ian S. Carr

(Opposite)
*By late 1964, Gateshead MPD had been largely reconstructed as a
servicing and maintenance depot, and steam was banished from the
new facilities. As if to emphasise that fact, No 60127* Wilson
Worsdell *stands dead amid dereliction at Gateshead on 25 May
1965, on the eve of the 'A1's' withdrawal.*
Ian S. Carr

longer had a regular working to London for its Pacifics.

Relatively few performance logs have survived featuring
Gateshead engine and men on their most familiar turns, not
surprisingly perhaps as these were sleeping car trains or
heavy trains with less capacity for the sort of running that set
the stop-watches clicking. O. S. Nock published details of a
trip in 1952 when he was on the footplate of No 60142

Edward Fletcher which was working the up 'Flying Scotsman' and at the head of a train of 440 ~~...~~ ~~...~~
~~...~~ ....Higginbotham of
Gateshead, and Nock commented that he had 'rarely seen a
locomotive handled with more precision and care, both from
the driver's and fireman's point of view'. The fireman
seemed a real expert in judging the use of the injector and in
firing, and boiler pressure was maintained at a consistent figure, just below blowing-off. No 60142 was driven with cut-
offs as short as 13%, usually with the regulator full open, but
on Cockburnspath bank the cut-off was advanced to 29%.

No high speeds were attained on this run and another
observer, Ian S, Carr, comments that in his experience the
standard of running north of Newcastle was usually adequate

for timekeeping, but not for copious recovery of time. He
~~...~~
with No 60135 *Madge Wildfire* on 12 bogies when he was
fireman to Maurice Rhodes, both of Gateshead. He
remarked that the engine was worked hard, being driven on
full regulator and with late cut-offs up the banks and 15%
on favourable stretches. The coal consumption in these conditions was at the rate of 60lb/mile.

Ian Carr recorded No 60127 *Wilson Worsdell* of Heaton in
February 1959 working the 2pm Kings Cross-Newcastle
when, after a late departure from York, the engine took 12
bogies, say, 400 tons, along the faintly rising grades north of
the city at 82-85 mph and cleared Cowton, 37 miles from the
start, in $32^3/_4$ min. On another run, this observer timed No

60154 *Bon Accord* of Gateshead on the seven-coach up 'Talisman' when an actual time of just under $257^1/_2$ min from Newcastle to Kings Cross saw 6min cut from the schedule, despite speeds nowhere higher than 78 mph, and a minimum speed up to Stoke summit of $55^1/_2$ mph.

The impression of the 'A1s' from all accounts in print, and at first hand, was that they were usually worked well within their capacity. Indeed, most of the schedules demanded no more than this. To get the most out of these Pacifics called for arduous work on the part of the fireman, hard-put to fill the 50 sq ft grate (Gresley Pacifics had 41 sq ft grates) and in keeping the back corners well-filled. Kings Cross driver, Bill Hoole once remarked to Kenneth Leech who was riding with him on an 'A1' that 'to drive this engine hard would knock the heart out of any fireman'. Andy Robson recalls being the driver on No 60129 *Guy Mannering* at the head of the 540ton down 'Aberdonian'. 'The fire was made up at Kings Cross shed, and I might add that the firebox was full. The first time that my fireman Jock Wilson picked up the shovel was beyond Huntingdon, some 60 miles from Kings Cross'.

Harry Friend summarises his view as a fireman of the 'A1s'

succinctly: 'Having an "A1" meant that I had to pile on more coal as compared, say, to a Gresley engine...and when run-down they were lively riders.' Their riding could be particularly bad at speeds over 80mph, and generally they were less happy when worked at shorter cut-offs of less than 15%. Andy Robson comments on the riding of the 'A1s' as follows: 'I suppose they were sometimes rough but being manned by three sets of men the engines were kept up to a fair standard. If one of them tended to slip at speed, it was sent to the main works for weighing and the springs adjusted accordingly. Another problem was that the coupling bars between engine and tender became stretched. This was rectified by the shed blacksmith who took the bars off and shortened them.'

Throughout the 1950s, the allocation of 17 'A1s' at Gateshead and Heaton remained almost as unchanging as the

Almost at its end, and shorn of its nameplates with their fine-sounding name of Guy Mannering, *No 60129 had been condemned for scrap just a week before it was photographed at Heaton shed on 18 October 1965.*

By then Gateshead had lost its steam allocation while Heaton had been closed to steam in 1963.
Ian S. Carr

pattern of the first-named shed's workings to London. The first alteration came in September 1956 with the introduction of the 'Talisman' express between Kings Cross and Edinburgh. Gateshead was responsible for working the up train whose engine returned north with the next day's 10.10am to Gla~~sgow. But~~

~~one of the shed's 'A1s' rather than an 'A1'~~, the Gresley engines then being progressively fitted with Kylchap exhausts and double chimneys.

With an extension of through engine and men's workings in the winter 1957 timetable, Grantham shed lost work to other sheds, notably Gateshead which now covered six up Newcastle-Kings Cross and return workings. Four in each direction were with overnight trains, the day turns - Sundays excepted - including the 8am from Newcastle and 5.35pm return, and the up 'Afternoon Talisman', in this case returning with the 10.10am Kings Cross-Glasgow. At this time, Gateshead engines were diagrammed to the 'Flying Scotsman' and 'North Briton' expresses between Newcastle and Edinburgh in each direction; as mentioned already, the latter pair of trains formed a fill-in turn for the engine allocated to the Kings Cross lodging turn. Other diagrams took the 'A1s' to Leeds and back at the head of Newcastle-Liverpool expresses, some of these being routed via the Coast line

Heaton covered the up and down 'Queen of Scots' in a diagram which took in the 7am Newcastle-Edinburgh (conveying sleeping cars from Kings Cross) and the 11.5pm from Edinburgh (the 'Aberdonian'). A Heaton Pacific was used on the up 'Northumbrian' to Peterborough, returning north with the overnight Colchester-Glasgow train as far as York, to regain Tyneside at the head of a parcels train.

The next changes presaged the dieselisation of the East Coast expresses which began in the winter 1958 timetable with the entry into service of the first 'English Electric' Type 4s from Hornsey depot. Although the total of six workings each way for the Gateshead Pacifics was unchanged, one or two workings were swapped, such that the 11am Kings Cross-Glasgow, 3pm Kings Cross-Newcastle and up and down 'Aberdonian' passed to the shed's engines and men. The 7.53am Sunderland-Kings Cross and 2pm Kings Cross-Newcastle were worked by a Gateshead engine north of Grantham.

That remained the position until further deliveries of 'English Electric' Type 4s began from 1959 when the end was in sight for regular Gateshead Pacific workings on the premier East Coast express trains. In preparation for the newcomers, a number of changes were made to Gateshead's facilities. Previous to this, from 1956 two of the depot's four roundhouses had been re-roofed and one was abandoned. Part of one shed was screened off for use by diesels and a new building provided for offices, staff facilities, machine shop and stores. The new shed was referred to as ~~Gateshead Greenfield and f~~ ~~driver and shed staff training.~~

From September 1960, there were 20 cyclic diagrams for 26 diesels, and of Gateshead's Pacifics the 'A1s' were the ones facing redundancy. Nos 60132/7/51 departed to Heaton in May 1960, to be followed four months later by Nos 60124/9/42/7/55. Finally, in November 1960 Nos 60115/35/45 were transferred to Copley Hill, and No 60154 to York, with the result that the shed was without a single 'A1'.

The rest of the story of the Tyneside 'A1s' is one of decline. From 1960 they found work from Heaton, but often off their home patch and usually on parcels, fitted freight and relief passenger trains. Then, in September 1962, came the transfer of these ten engines to Tweedmouth. In December 1964, Gateshead renewed its acquaintance with some of its earlier 'A1' allocation when the shed received Nos 60116/27/9/32/42/51, together with Nos 60117/48 previously allocated to West Riding sheds. Relatively little employment was available for the 'A1s', often no more than working Control specials of empty wagons along the main line. By 14 March 1965, Nos 60116/27/9/32/42/51 were put to store, all but Nos 60129/51 being condemned on 14 June. Nos 60129/51 eked out a twilight existence until later that year, after allocation to York.

Still seeing action into 1965 were former Gateshead engines, Nos 60124/45, and they were employed as main line pilots, the former at Darlington. As a driver, Harry Friend encountered the former during the summer of 1965 when it was the only engine available to work a bulk cement train forward from Skelton, York to Tyne Yard. No 60124 set off with 1,000 tons behind her. 'I opened the regulator fully, got her to 45mph, then ran with half-regulator and the cut-off at 20% - no bother at all. The "A1" was much more powerful than a Type 4 diesel...'

And so the 'A1s', Gateshead and otherwise, departed from the scene. The Tyneside shed got some of the best from them but, in trying to summarise the attitudes of crews towards these Pacifics, it seems curiously difficult to reach a definite verdict. 'Coal-eaters', rough riders, certainly; good performers from the point of view of main works, shed running staffs and operating men, most certainly, but there is a distinct feeling that 'on the road' they were respected but not loved.

5

NINE ELMS AND THE PACKETS
running the 'Merchant Navies'

London's last steam shed was Nine Elms, and accounts of its later days are inseparable from the controversy surrounding the Bulleid Pacifics and their rebuilding.

A half-century later, the atmosphere of early postwar London, with its dilapidation, shortages, weariness and bomb-sites is as far-distant as that of the capital known to Charles Dickens. Much of that era was epitomised by Nine Elms shed. Similarly remote is the contemporary impact of the heralds of a new, postwar world. On the railway scene, 'herald' was fitting description of the Bulleid Pacifics. True, the early 'Merchant Navies' had been introduced in the darkest days of wartime, and even delivery of the second series, Nos 21C11-20, only just overlapped VE-Day. Most of this batch were to stay at Nine Elms for the next couple of decades.

The ten engines entered traffic in an unrelieved black paintwork but, before long, were re-liveried in the glowing malachite green with parallel yellow bands that was a powerful antidote to the environmental drabness of Nine Elms - and Waterloo station. At the head of the polished Pullman cars of the 'Bournemouth Belle', reintroduced in October 1946, or those of the 'Devon Belle' of 1947, the result was one of the m~

~~~ the late wartime 'baby boom', the alluring image of the 'Packets' has remained with them ever since.

At Nine Elms, Nos 21C11-20 replaced ten of the 'Nelsons' which went to Bournemouth and, once acclimatised to their new charges, the enginemen became enthusiastic supporters. Associated with these Pacifics from new, the late Bert Hooker has written, 'there wasn't an outstanding one, nor a "dud" in the batch. They were all "good'uns" but, of course, each crew considered "their" engine a cut above the rest'...'these engines would run and run with the boilers providing an apparently limitless amount of steam. The riding qualities were superb...'

Of that allocation, and by now renumbered, Nos 35017- 9 and their Nine Elms crews represented the Southern Region during the 1948 Exchange Trials. No 35017 *Belgian Marine* worked between Euston and Carlisle, and Kings Cross and Leeds, and No 35019 *French Line CGT* between Paddington and Plymouth. Nine Elms' drivers James, Snell, Swain

and their firemen, including the late Bert Hooker, featured in the working of these and the Light Pacifics 'on tour'. No 35018 *British India Line* remained on its home ground, with No 35020 *Bibby Line* as spare.

In the design of the Pacifics, Bulleid included a number of features that not only appealed to enginemen, but made their work easier. Much that has been written about the Pacifics

(Opposite)
Epitomising its role as 'a herald' of the postwar railway era, No 21C13 Blue Funnel, *in SR malachite green livery, waits to leave Waterloo on 15 July 1947 with the down 'Bournemouth Belle' which formed the outward leg of Nine Elms Duty No 35.*
John P. Wilson/Rail Archive Stephenson

(Below)
The 'Devon Belle' was a prestigious working, but by the early 1950s it attracted limited patronage, and the train ceased running with the end of the 1954 summer timetable. In this picture dated Monday, 4 July 1949, the 'Belle' has left Waterloo at midday and No 35012 United States Lines *is seen passing the former Gas Light and Coke Company works at Nine Elms which hemmed in the railway land to the north of the main line. The wagons to the left of the picture are in Nine Elms goods depot which sprawled both sides of the main lines.*
John P. Wilson/Rail Archive Stephenson

by enginemen's enthusiasm. Conversely, some of the unfavourable verdicts cast on the Bulleid originals have come from maintenance staff and management. Those involved in the rebuilding process can hardly be expected to take a disinterested stance.

Nearly 30 years after the Bulleid Pacifics ceased work on BR, controversy has neither abated nor loyalties lessened. This says something about a fundamental aspect of the steam engineman - his craft. Bulleid's Pacifics were a creation that epitomised what enginemen felt about their calling, and to some extent the Southern men identified with the engines. These, the feeling went, were so good - on top form - that 'They' = the Management had to interfere with them. The working boiler pressure was reduced from 1952-4. This, combined with the rebuilding process from 1956, was seen by many enginemen as combining to rob the engines of their potency. Some enginemen contended that rebuilding was an unnecessary expense.

Commentators may say that such opinions add up to no more than misplaced loyalty. Yet, although there is well-documented evidence that rebuilding made the engines cheaper to run, the case for retention of the original concept of the Pacifics continues to be advanced cogently by those involved with them at the 'sharp end'. That includes enginemen and fitters alike, and, it may be said, those with recent experience of an unmodified Pacific on the main line, such as the Keigh-

No 35014 Nederland Line *is on Bournemouth shed on 16 September 1950, and displaying cladding in poor condition and grubby malachite livery. Bulleid said that in order to save weight lighter than desirable steel sheeting had to be used for the casing of the 'Merchant Navies'. This engine was never painted blue and during 1951 received BR Brunswick green livery. Note that it has been modified with a wedge-shaped cab front. Close inspection reveals that the engine is carrying the 'Bournemouth Belle' headboard, and no doubt it has just worked the down train.*
Wm Rogerson/Rail Archive Stephenson

ley and Worth Valley Railway's sponsors of Light Pacific No 34092 *City of Wells*.

To return to Nine Elms, a locomotive depot was first built there with the opening in 1838 of the earliest section of the London & Southampton Railway. Its location was on the 'river' side of the line, and remained so after the closure in 1848 of Nine Elms terminus to regular passenger traffic and until 1865, by which time part of the station also had been adapted as another engine shed. A third depot was built in 1865 on the (then) south side of the running lines into Waterloo, but a bold plan in the late 1870s saw these realigned to the south, with the line of the new viaduct enforcing removal of the locomotive depot.

The site for the fourth depot was well to the south of the realigned main lines, and to the west of the locomotive, carriage and wagon works, themselves relocated in 1865 from

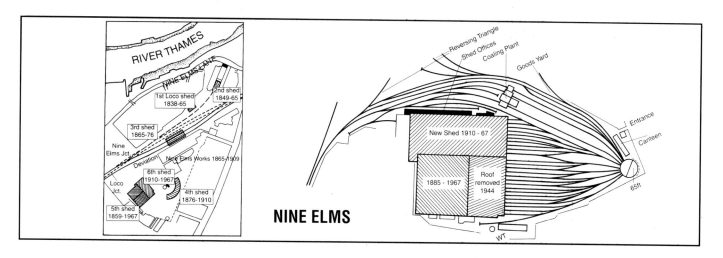

NINE ELMS

No 35020 Bibby Line *was no more than a month out of Eastleigh Works after rebuilding when photographed on its home shed in late May 1956. It had been paired with 6,000-gallon tender No T3345 with the original high side sheeting, in preparation for the controlled road test on the West of England line for assessment of the rebuilt engines.*

J. F. Davies/Rail Archive Stephenson

the area of the original Nine Elms terminus. This fourth shed dated from 1876, and comprised a semi-circular roundhouse, with twin turntables, accompanied by an imposing office building. Splendid though these facilities were, they soon needed enlargement to cope with larger engines. One feature of the shed's location was to dog operations into and out of Waterloo until the end of steam. Access to the main line was

from Loco Junction where there was a trailing connection with the running lines, and this required the reversal of all locomotives working into and out of Waterloo.

Further accommodation was needed at Nine Elms for burgeoning freight traffic, and this contributed to the London & South Western Railway's decision to relocate its locomotive, carriage and wagon works to Eastleigh. The process started in 1890, and was completed in 1910. The running shed also suffered from this expansion of the freight depot, and its semi-roundhouse was accordingly sacrificed so that yet another replacement was constructed that year; this was a 'straight' shed alongside another such which dated from the mid-1880s. There were now covered facilities on 25 roads, and a coaling stage, the latter being replaced in 1932 by a mechanical coaling plant.

In this form, Nine Elms shed was to remain little changed for the rest of the steam age, apart from the attentions of the Luftwaffe which left the shed roofs badly damaged, and other depredations. Even after piecemeal repairs, to put it mildly the depot remained derelict-looking, and schemes for rebuilding were repeatedly shelved.

Before the first stage of electrifying the suburban passenger services from Waterloo, Nine Elms had an allocation of 150 engines. By the time Pacifics Nos 21C11-20 had arrived

at the depot that total had gradually reduced to 114. The latest arrivals were for premier duties on the Bournemouth and West of England expresses but the depot's responsibilities also encompassed special and semi-fast passenger trains, main line and local freight turns from Nine Elms Goods, and the yard shunters there, as well as empty stock workings

(Below)
The turntable at Nine Elms shed was at the extremity of the depot, and all 25 shed roads converged on it. By the time that No 35005 Canadian Pacific was photographed on 15 June 1957 posing on the turntable, the familiar block of flats had been completed, a landmark of the shed's environs. The engine is carrying a disc for Special 106 duty. It would not have been first choice for Nine Elms' premier duties by then, and is just a fortnight away from works attention at Eastleigh; not until April 1959 did No 35005 arrive at Eastleigh for rebuilding.
J. F. Davies/Rail Archive Stephenson

(Opposite)
Exmouth Junction shed's No 35023 Holland-Afrika Line *on shed at Nine Elms, 26 May 1956. The engine is standing outside the 15-road shed built in 1885 which lost part of its roof during World War 2, and is alongside the New Shed of 1910.*
J. F. Davies/Rail Archive Stephenson

between Clapham Junction carriage sidings (and elsewhere) and Waterloo.

On allocation to Nine Elms, the ten 'Merchant Navies' were double-manned by Top Link crews. During the 1940s, they worked no further west than Bournemouth and Salisbury, all through trains being re-engined at these stations, and the locomotives being worked out and back by the same crew. The exception was the summer-only 'Devon Belle' which passed Salisbury without stopping, only to change engines at Wilton. Engine changing was discontinued in 1950, and then the engines went through to Exeter, the Nine Elms men being relieved by, or taking over at Salisbury from an Exmouth Junction or Salisbury crew. While apparently in the interests of productivity, the change from double manning to common-user working was detrimental to the Pacifics which had benefited from the allocation of two sets of men only to each locomotive. Pride in the job suffered as a result, as well-remembered by Southern men with experi-

ence of that period. The 'Devon Belle' continued to change engines at Wilton, except in the summer of 1954 when the Pacific on the Friday afternoon working from Waterloo continued to Exeter. In this case, water was taken at Salisbury where a stop was scheduled.

In 1949, the lengthened wartime schedules had been tightened up somewhat, but the West of England expresses did not see appreciable cuts in timings until the summer 1952 timetable. Then the 'Atlantic Coast Express' was significantly accelerated, to a 3hr 16min overall time westbound to Exeter, and four minutes slower eastbound. These changes introduced a 60mph booking between Waterloo and Salisbury, and exacting timings in each direction between Salisbury and Sidmouth Junction. By now, the sometimes gargantuan loads of wartime and just-postwar days - not unusually 16/17 coaches - had given way to 12/13 coaches.

On the Bournemouth line, fastest train was the 'Bournemouth Belle', in 130min to Bournemouth Central,

and 5min faster back to Waterloo; the tighter timing that had applied initially on the train's restoration had been eased. The Pacifics did not have matters all the own way as from 1953-5 diesels Nos 10000/1 and 10201-3 were used on both the Western Section main lines, to Exeter, and to Bournemouth and Weymouth. During this period, all 'Merchant Navies' were temporarily withdrawn for examination of their coupled axles following the failure of the driving axle of Nine Elms' No 35020 at Crewkerne in April 1953. The shed received a varied allocation of stand-ins, ranging from 'Britannia' Pacifics and ex-LNER 'V2' 2-6-2s to ex-LMS and BR '5' 4-6-0s and ex-LNER 'B1' 4-6-0s.

By now, proposals were being hatched for the rebuilding of the Bulleid Pacifics along more conventional lines, and in January 1955 the CM&EE of the Southern Region issued a report which has received publicity a number of times. The case for rebuilding was justified, so the report said, because it 'would virtually eliminate the principal troublesome features and bring the running costs into line with those of the

other leading express passenger locomotives without impairing their performance in any way...' Of that more anon, but the first engine for modification was Nine Elms No 35018 which was outshopped in its altered form in February 1956.

Meanwhile, from 3 May 1954, there had been changes to the Top Link duties on the Bournemouth line, with the introduction of through engine workings to/from Weymouth. The principal turns for Nine Elms are included in Table 1, the changes in general aiming to increase through workings by the depot's engines. Only on Duty No 33 which covered the working of the 'Bournemouth Belle' each way did a Nine Elms crew return with the engine they had taken west earlier in the day. The Bournemouth engines were also remanned for their return home, that depot's engine turns also being simple 'out and back' workings. Dorchester shed covered two workings to/from Waterloo, for which until September 1954 it was allocated two 'Nelsons'. Some involved with the Pacifics saw the 1954 re-diagramming as yet another example of deteriorating operating standards.

On the West of England trains, there continued to be out and return workings of Nine Elms Pacifics to Exeter, with a change of crew at Salisbury in each direction. While the engine heading the 9am from Waterloo to Exeter came back with the 4.30pm departure from Exeter Central, other diagrams for Nine Elms Pacifics affirmed their original role as mixed traffic engines, as return east was made with milk or fitted freight trains.

The process of rebuilding the 'Merchant Navies' progressed such that, by June 1957, Nine Elms had Nos 35012/4/6/7/8/20, as well as unmodified Nos 35005/19/29/30, the last two of these having come from the Eastern Section. With five rebuilt engines at Bournemouth in addition, from the summer June 1957 timetable the Southern Region seemed at last confident of reintroducing two-hour schedules between Waterloo and Bournemouth Central, at 8.20, 10.30am and 6.30pm down, and with the 12.40, 2.40, 6.40 and 7.40pm up departures, the last-noted being a summer-only train. The rebuilt engines accordingly

(Opposite)
Nine Elms' No 35030 Elder-Dempster Lines *on the shed's Duty No 6 which covered the down 'Atlantic Coast Express', photographed near Templecombe on 6 September 1963. Erstwhile Southern operating standards were deteriorating by this time, and the 'ACE' had lost some of its through portions but at least the engine is carrying a headboard. No 35030 was outshopped from what was to be its last general overhaul in May 1962, and went to Eastleigh for a Heavy Intermediate overhaul in November 1963.*
D. M. C. Hepburne-Scott/Rail Archive Stephenson

(Above)
No 35012 United States Lines *approaches Woking with an up Bournemouth express on 13 September 1964, the Sunday after the introduction of the winter 1964/5 timetable which brought the end of steam working of Waterloo-West of England expresses, and the transfer of Bulleid Pacifics away from Nine Elms. Note the leading Bulleid corridor second S43S, one of those that has had its external panelling renewed.*
Brian Stephenson

dominated the working of the two-hour trains during the first months of the new timetable although unmodified engines were by no means unknown. In the Nine Elms' Top Link of the time, to take four names at random, were Drivers Chant, Hooper, Letchford and Roberts. Sample diagrams dating from winter 1959/60 are given in Table 2; as compared with 1954, Nine Elms had ceded some workings to Bournemouth shed.

The West of England expresses were as yet not greatly altered, apart from the isolated acceleration in the summer 1957 timetable of the 4.30pm from Exeter, retimed to reach Waterloo 19min earlier. With introduction as from September 1957 of new expresses on the route, at 6.30am from Exeter to Waterloo, and 7pm return, the workings on the route for engines and men were redrafted, and for a while the new trains were headed by Nine Elms engines. Apart from Exmouth Junction shed, Salisbury also contributed to haulage of the Waterloo-West of England expresses, as its engines covered the 2.30pm from Exeter Central, and, from

September 1957, the 1pm down from Waterloo. By the late 1950s, winter weekdays diagrams for Nine Elms engines on the service were as shown in Table 3, and these may be taken as typical. From late July to early September, the 'ACE' ran in two portions east of Exeter each weekday while summer Saturdays saw the operation of numerous additional holiday trains. One variation in the winter 1961/2 timetable was that the Nine Elms engine off the down 'ACE' remained at Exmouth Junction to work the next day's up 'ACE'.

A later addition to the West of England expresses was the Surbiton-Okehampton car carrier train which ran during the summers of 1960-4 inclusive, worked by Nine Elms engines

Upon rebuilding, the class-leader, No 35001 Channel Packet, *returned to the Western Division and not long afterwards is seen approaching Seaton Junction with the down 'Atlantic Coast Express' of 23 September 1959. The top headcode disc indicates that the engine is working on Nine Elms' Diagram 6.*
K. L. Cook/Rail Archive Stephenson

In this 1964 photograph, No 35012 United States Lines *winds the down 'Atlantic Coast Express' through Clapham Junction with its speed-restricted platform lines.*
Brian Stephenson

to and from Exeter. The summer 1961 timetable featured the overdue acceleration of the up 'ACE' to a mile-a-minute timing between Salisbury and Waterloo, and then came further cuts in timings to the down and up 'ACEs' alike in the winter 1961/2 timetable: journey times were 178min westbound to Exeter, and 1min slower coming up. Over the $83^3/_4$ miles between Waterloo and Salisbury, the 'ACE' was now running to 80min bookings each way, by then undoubtedly the hardest passenger train schedules on BR still regularly entrusted to steam.

Over the next couple of years, recorders with stopwatches recorded for posterity many notable runs with Nine Elms engines and crews, but time was running out for steam trac-

tion generally. Yet, as late as September 1962, the SR management was still contemplating electrification to Bournemouth co-existing with Pacific working of the West of England expresses. Under this plan, Nine Elms would have retained an allocation of Pacifics and its facilities would have been rationalised to comprise the triangle, Nos 1/2 disposal pit roads, the turntable, coaling facilities and staff block. Regional boundary changes imposed by the British Railways Board soon put paid to thoughts of an outpost of Southern steam, and ushered in plans for a truncated express service running between Exeter and Waterloo only, with diesel motive power provided by the Western Region.

Phil Bassett remembers the atmosphere of the time at Nine Elms. 'By 1963 the engines were mostly on a wing and a prayer, but the skill of the examining fitters, armed with acetylene lamp and hammer, ensured that the fleet was kept in safe running condition.' In November 1963, Nine Elms' allocation of 'Merchant Navies' comprised Nos 35001/12/4-20/4/8-30 but, within a couple of months, withdrawals of the

TABLE 1
Nine Elms '8P' diagrams on the Bournemouth line, as from 3 May 1954

Duty No	Train
30	2.40am Waterloo-Bournemouth Central newspaper train 7.20am Bournemouth West-Waterloo
31	5.40am Waterloo-Weymouth 1.25pm Weymouth-Waterloo
32	8.30am Waterloo-Weymouth 5.35pm Weymouth-Waterloo
33	12.30pm 'Bournemouth Belle', Waterloo-Bournemouth West 4.30pm 'Bournemouth Belle' Bournemouth West-Waterloo
34	9.30am Waterloo-Bournemouth West 3.5pm Bournemouth West-Waterloo
35	10.30am Waterloo-Weymouth 6.30pm Weymouth-Waterloo
36	4.35pm 'Royal Wessex', Waterloo-Weymouth 9.55pm Weymouth-Waterloo

TABLE 2
Principal Nine Elms '8P' diagrams on the Bournemouth line winter 1959/60 timetable

Trains

8.20am SX Waterloo-Bournemouth West*
1pm Bournemouth West-Waterloo (worked SX)

10.30am Waterloo-Weymouth*
5.35pm Weymouth-Waterloo*

2.30am Waterloo-Bournemouth Central newspaper train
7.20am Bournemouth West-Waterloo
7pm Waterloo-Exeter Central

Trains with a 2hr schedule to/from Bournemouth Central

TABLE 3
Principal Nine Elms '8P' diagrams on the West of England line late 1950s

Duty No	Trains
5	9am Waterloo-Exeter Central 4.30pm Exeter Central-Waterloo
6	11am 'Atlantic Coast Express', Waterloo-Exeter Central 6.48pm milk train Exeter Central-Clapham Junction
7	3pm Waterloo-Exeter Central 10.42pm express fitted freight Exeter Central yard-Nine Elms

class had begun. The shed's No 35015 was one of the first to be condemned. Next followed dieselisation of the Waterloo-Exeter expresses with the winter 1964/5 timetable, coincident with which Nine Elms lost all its Pacific allocation, the 'Merchant Navies' going to Weymouth, with the exception of No 35001/22, both of which were transfered to Bournemouth. To cover morning down expresses from Waterloo, a couple of 'Merchant Navies' from the other depots were stabled overnight at Nine Elms.

In the last years of steam working at Nine Elms there were 12 sets of men in the Top Link: eight running and four spare turns. The enginemen continued to uphold the proud traditions of their shed, even if it lacked its own Pacifics. Although fast running in the final summer of SR steam working has generally attracted more attention, some excellent performances were recorded in 1965, as well as later, notably by Drivers Anderson, Hendicott, Hooper, Porter and Saunders. Almost at the end, in April 1967 Pacifics returned to Nine Elms' allocation and, with the demise of Southern steam, Nos 35007/8/13/23/8/30 were condemned on shed.

The Southern Region engine record cards held by the Public Record Office at Kew are disappointing on three counts: the records start only at 1952/3; the mileages between classified repairs are not included as is the case with some other Regions' records, and the cards are missing for Nos 35014/7/20 of the series allocated new to Nine Elms during 1945.

Details from the record cards for Nos 35012 and 35018 are given in Table 4. These show that, whatever might be said about the heavy maintenance requirements of the engines in their original form, the frequency of works' visits to Eastleigh Works was not markedly different before and after rebuilding. In 'as-built' condition, a general overhaul took some 30-40 days, and although in later days a general overhaul on a 'Merchant Navy' was scheduled to take no more 22 working days from arrival to dispatch some of the improvement was down to more efficient repair methods. A general overhaul involved a boiler lift and its replacement, complete stripping down of motion and valve gear, and the wheels dropped. Nor were annual mileages much different after rebuilding; some engines achieved higher figures before conversion.

In either form, the Pacifics did not compare unfavourably with other Regions' express passenger types when it came to the time spent in works for general overhauls. The smart turnaround of engines in for rebuilding is worth noting. Although most of the replacement components were manufactured by Eastleigh, other BR works were also involved in their production. A 'kit of parts' was set out ready when the engine scheduled for rebuilding came into works.

As to the nature of repairs and defects experienced with the 'Merchant Navies', fitters with first-hand knowledge of the engines in both versions are ready to point out that some defects were easier to rectify in original form. Although the Bulleid chain-driven valve gear has been criticised on a number of scores, John Churchill, a fitter at Yeovil Junction and

TABLE 4
Details from BR (SR) Engine record cards of Nine Elms 'Merchant Navies'
Nos 35012 and 35018

No 35012 *United States Lines* Built January 1945, withdrawn April 1967

Overhaul catergory		Into Works	Outshopped
In original condition			
General	Eastleigh	6/5/52	5/7/52
Light Casual*	Eastleigh	4/6/53	12/6/53
Heavy Intermediate	Eastleigh	20/11/53	19/12/53
Light Intermediate	Eastleigh	23/12/54	22/1/55
Light Intermediate	Eastleigh	20/1/56	18/2/56
*Driving axle replaced after inspection			
As rebuilt			
General/modification	Eastleigh	25/1/57	28/2/57
Light Casual	Eastleigh	4/12/57	21/12/57
Light Intermediate	Eastleigh	2/12/58	24/12/58
Non-classified	Eastleigh	27/10/59	7/11/59
Light Casual	Exmouth Jct	9/12/59	18/1/60
Heavy Intermediate	Eastleigh	11/8/60	3/9/60
General	Eastleigh	7/3/62	21/4/62
Light Casual	Eastleigh	11/10/62	27/10/62
Light Casual	Eastleigh	17/5/63	1/6/63
Light Intermediate	Eastleigh	26/2/64	18/4/64
Casual	Eastleigh	29/7/64	19/8/64

Transferred to Weymouth shed period ending 14 September 1964

| Light Casual | Eastleigh | 11/2/66 | 10/3/66 |

Transferred to Nine Elms shed period endidng 17 April 1967

No 35018 *British India Line* Built March 1945, withdrawn August 1964. Preserved on Mid-Hants Railway

Overhaul category		Into Works	Outshopped
Casual	Eastleigh	10/6/52	4/7/52
Non-classified	Eastleigh	7/7/52	11/7/52
Light Casual	Eastleigh	29/9/52	14/10/52
Light Intermediate	Eastleigh	8/4/53	2/5/53
Light Casual*	Eastleigh	4/6/53	12/6/53
Light Casual	Eastleigh	2/12/53	16/12/53
Heavy Intermediate	Eastleigh	28/6/54	7/8/54
*Driving axle replaced			
As Rebuilt			
General/modification	Eastleigh	16/11/55	14/2/56
Non-classified	Eastleigh	16/4/56	17/4/56
Valve & Piston Exam	Brighton	25/9/56	4/10/56
Light Casual	Eastleigh	8/3/57	13/3/57
Light Intermediate	Eastleigh	14/5/58	14/6/58
Non-classified	Eastleigh	24/4/59	8/5/59
Light Intermediate	Eastleigh	14/1/60	6/2/60
Non-classified	Eastleigh	2/12/60	10/12/60
General	Eastleigh	7/11/61	13/1/62
Non-classified	Eastleigh	10/4/62	19/4/62
Light Casual	Bricklayers Arms	17/5/63	12/7/63
Light Casual	Eastleigh	23/8/63	7/9/63

No 35029 Ellerman Lines *was on Weymouth shed's allocation when photographed near Hinton Admiral with the down 'Bournemouth Belle' on 18 September 1965. This engine went for scrapping at Woodhams, Barry but was subsequently acquired for display in sectioned form at the National Railway Museum.*
D. M. C. Hepburne-Scott/Rail Archive Stephenson

Salisbury sheds, and who completed his apprenticeship at Eastleigh Works, comments:

> Many features on the unmodified engines were easier to repair in situ than when Walschaerts valve gear was fitted, or indeed as compared with the Maunsell designs. Despite what has often been said, the Morse drive chains did not often suffer breakages - in most cases what was required was to insert new links, and that could be done without removing the chains. Nor was the leakage of oil from the oil-bath that serious - most of the leakage came from the motion. The Hadfield steam reversers did provide us with problems but the design itself was not at fault: the reversers crept because the washers in the hydraulic system deteriorated. Even so, topping up the hydraulic cylinder with oil usually did the trick, and that was done by fitters - like me - at stations. When it came to stripping down an unrebuilt Pacific on shed, that took extra time because of the number of bolts that needed to be taken out on each panel of the air-smoothed casing, and the work required in taking down the oil sump.

Bulleid is on record as saying that the answer would have been to provide the casing in the form of hinged covers to each side of the engine, to be lifted up like the bonnet of a motor car.

Enginemen's judgments of the Pacifics before and after rebuilding have been recorded for posterity, thanks to the efforts during 1966/7 of Mr G. Harrison of Salisbury. Crews were normally disinclined to put pen to paper, although seldom shy when vocalising their praise or distaste of engines - or management. To working (and retired) enginemen from his local depot, and also at Exmouth Junction and Nine Elms, Mr Harrison circulated a testimonial drafted by Driver Pistell of Salisbury. It read: 'We the undersigned having had considerable experience in working the "Merchant Navy", "Battle of Britain" and "West Country" locomotives both in their original and modified condition, are in no doubt that the best performance and free-running were obtained when they were in their original condition.'

Of those receiving the testimonial card, 108 signed and returned the card sent to Mr Harrison. Just one dissenter did not endorse Driver Pistell's remarks.

Overwhelmingly, the comments volunteered by drivers were in favour of the chain-driven valve gear on the grounds that it was lighter in weight, and that the increased resistance of the Walschaerts valve gear had reduced the free-running characteristics of the engines as rebuilt, as well as worsening the quality of ride and inducing axlebox knock. Whatever might be said to disprove such verdicts, when offered independently by drivers from three sheds, including retired men, too, they cannot be brushed aside. Also, some drivers made reference to the increased time required to prepare the rebuilt engines, and the awkwardness of oiling round. Disadvantages of the unmodified engines were listed as the poor lockout from the cab, and problems with the reverser; some drivers considered that operation of the screw reverser fitted to the rebuilds required an appreciable physical effort.

Signed testimonial cards were returned from comparatively few Nine Elms drivers, the initiative having originated at Salisbury and Exmouth Junction. Although Bulleid was personally delighted at the quantity and tone of the annotated testimonial cards which were duly presented to him, he cautioned Alan Wilton, Secretary of the Bulleid Pacific Preservation Society, against publicising a further testimonial to be organised among Nine Elms drivers 'as some of the people responsible for the rebuilding are still quite influential at HQ'.

Of those drivers at Nine Elms who had responded to the first testimonial, a range of comments accompanied the cards: Driver G. Holloway - 'the rebuilds were a step backwards in locomotive progress'; H. Pope, who fired on No 35014 when new, 'Alterations affected the freedom of running and riding. Retarded their performance'; Henry Sartin, with 50 years railway service, 'You (referring to Bulleid) built... the Rolls of locomotion'; S. Emm, 'Alterations detrimental'; F. Cutting, 'in 49 years at Nine Elms... the best engines for performance were the MN and WC class as built'.

Much more could be said on the subject, but the extracts included above are offered as an insight into the views of the enginemen of Nine Elms who had worked with the ten 'Merchant Navies' (and the other Pacifics) so long associated with the shed. Its latter-day heyday with the 'Belles' and the 'ACE' took the story of steam to its sunset, not only at Waterloo but in London and the south of England.

6

'THE TALK OF THE LINE'
Barrow Road's 'Jubilees'

This chapter features a proud outpost of the Midland, and later the LMS, whose engines worked cross-country expresses and which in BR days was particularly noted for its 'Jubilees'

The Midland and LMS both regarded the West of England main line from Birmingham to Bristol as less important than south from Derby to St Pancras. That said, there were some smartly-timed expresses over the West of England route before 1914. During the early 1920s, in the recovery from the extended timings of World War 1, matters gradually improved but it was 1933 before schedules were speeded-up on the LMS cross-country expresses between Bristol and Derby and beyond. The most notable timings were made by four trains daily which ran between Cheltenham and Bromsgrove - where a stop was made for banking

(Opposite)
Barrow Road's No 45577 Bengal *clatters over Mangotsfield North Junction with the 7.40am Bristol Temple Meads-Bradford Forster Square express in June 1956.*
George Heiron

(Above)
No 45690 Leander *is no doubt emitting the characteristic 'Jubilee' roar as it heads a Bradford Forster Square-Bristol Temple Meads express near Standish Junction during July 1953. Alongside are the metals of the ex-GWR route from Swindon and Stroud.*
George Heiron

assistance up the Lickey incline - in 31min for the 31.1 miles. Similarly smart was a fast 31min timing between Mangotsfield and Gloucester, later eased to 33min.

At this stage, Midland and LMS Compound 4-4-0s were the usual motive power but, by late 1934, LMS '5X' 4-6-0s were in use on the line, usually in the shape of what later became known as 'Patriots'. These hailed from Holbeck shed but, soon after, Barrow Road received a short-lived alloca-

tion of '5Xs', including taper boiler No 5662. At the beginning of 1938, Black Fives and Compounds constituted the shed's premier express power.

Plans were afoot to use the '5Xs' to speed-up the cross-country expresses and, in mid-October 1937, a remarkable four-day trial run was staged using 'Jubilee' No 5660 *Rooke*, working from Bristol to Leeds and Glasgow and back. This was seemingly intended to provide a bench-mark for new schedules over the route. At 98 years of age and still taking a lively interest in railway matters, former Barrow Road driver, Tom King, knew the Bristol enginemen involved in working *Rooke*.

Ted Gardner was the driver, and Percy Hook, the fireman, with Derby Inspector Harry Fowkes with them on No 5660. Ted let Fowkes dictate how the engine should be worked - full regulator and 35% on the rack. What was worse, he had the fireman work the front damper so that too much air was admitted to the grate. Percy had 200 miles of hammering, and No 5660 burnt over a quarter more coal per mile between Bristol and Leeds

than it did when worked by Holbeck men through to Glasgow. Shortly after the 1937 trials, Percy Hook died and No 5660 became known as the 'Killer'.

Although No 5660's test runs have been described as among the classics of steam performance, over some sections the engine was driven impossibly hard. Such efforts could not be sustained in normal service, such as over the 206 miles from Bristol to Leeds, and careful judgment on handling was required, given the number of intermediate stops, their effect on management of the fire by the fireman, and economical use of coal and water. This chapter takes as its main theme the attempts to diagram steam locomotives to lengthy through express workings, and how practicable it was.

Barrow Road shed was in the Lawrence Hill area of Bristol, situated in the fork of the running lines between Mangotsfield and Temple Meads, and those leading to the MR terminus at St Philips. The depot was dominated by the bridge carrying Barrow Road diagonally over the railway.

The depot featured a Midland brick-built roundhouse, the

usual style of Midland coaling stage, and stores and repair facilities, including sheer-legs for lifting engines. The well-equipped lifting and repair shop was at the rear of the round-house, and until 1949/50 came under direct control of the chief mechanical engineer's department at Derby. Thereafter, the shop passed to the control of the running shed.

From 1933, the LMS had progressively modernised its locomotive depots with the object of reducing the time expended on servicing locomotives, and usually this was accompanied by the provision of a mechanised coaling plant and modern a vacuum-operated turntable. The modernisation of Barrow Road during 1938/9 included the building of mechanised coaling and ash disposal plants, and the provision of a wheel-drop, the process involving replacement of the coaling stage.

Under the LMS's 1935 reorganisation of motive power depots, the shed had become a Main Depot for a district that took in the sheds at Gloucester, Bath, Templecombe and Highbridge, and it was the location of the district locomotive superintendent's office. Its LMS shed-code was 22A

which was retained by BR until 1958. The shed was typical with its sense of family, says Don Flook, at Barrow Road during the 1940s and 1950s as an apprentice fitter, and later fitter . Many of the staff had either themselves or had relatives who worked on the Somerset & Dorset Joint line. When Highbridge Works had closed in 1930 some of its staff transferred to the Melton Constable Works of the Midland & Great Northern Joint line. When in turn the LNER closed that works for locomotive repairs in 1936, some of these exiles took up vacancies at Barrow Road and other depots in its district.

In November 1945, Barrow Road's locomotive allocation totalled 66 and included the following 'Jubilees':

5557 *New Brunswick*	5627 *Sierra Leone*
5590 *Travancore*	5629 *Straits Settlements*
5612 *Jamaica*	5652 *Hawke*
5618 *New Hebrides*	5657 *Tyrwhitt*
5622 *Nyasaland*	5665 *Lord Rutherford of Nelson*

(Opposite)
Photographed from the overbridge, this is how Bristol Barrow Road shed appeared in the late 1950s, by which time it had begun to receive ex-GWR engines on its allocation with the transfer of control to the Western Region. Of the two 'Jubilees' visible on shed, furthest left is Holbeck's No 45568 Western Australia, *and making a move is the home shed's No 45690* Leander.
George Heiron

(Above)
A view from the first level of the coaling plant on a sultry, sulphurous summer afternoon in 1954. Past Barrow Road MPD comes a Derby-bound express while a '4F' 0-6-0 moves towards the shed from the ash-disposal plant, leaving ashes smouldering in the skip in the pit. LMS Compound 4-4-0 No 41064 awaits its next turn: in front of it is a 16-ton mineral wagon on the stop-block road gradually being loaded with spillages from locomotives being coaled at the plant. Once full, the wagon's contents will be loaded into the coal hopper.
D. T. Flook

These engines had tenders with 3,500-gallon capacity water tanks, and some with limited coal capacity. In view of the long through turns worked by the Barrow Road engines, the 1945 allocation was in time displaced by engines paired with larger capacity tenders which held 4,000 gallons of water and nine tons of coal. For example, No 5690 *Leander* was sent on loan from Crewe North depot in September 1947, and its permanent allocation was effected a month later.

By May 1951, the shed's tally of 'Jubilees' was as follows:

45561 *Saskatchewan*	45663 *Jervis*
45570 *New Zealand*	45682 *Trafalgar*
45572 *Eire*	45685 *Barfleur*
45660 *Rooke*	45690 *Leander*
45662 *Kempenfelt*	45699 *Galatea*

Although further changes were to take place, essentially this remained the basic allocation during the 1950s. By January 1954, Nos 45570 had gone, but its loss was outweighed by newcomers Nos 45577 *Bengal*, 45602 *British Honduras* and 45651 *Shovell*. Changes made to Regional boundaries from February 1958 affected the Birmingham-Bristol main line. As a result, the '22' motive power district was abolished, and Barrow Road and its sub-depots were transferred to the Western Region, with overall responsibility passing to Bris-

And this is what the environs of Barrow Road MPD looked like from the top floor of the coaling plant. Across the site runs the 'Barrow Road Bridge', as it was known by locals and generations of locospotters alike. Washing and rhubarb belonging to residents of the houses in Robert Street - to the left of the picture - fight a losing battle with the ashes, coal dust and fumes from the depot. A northbound double-headed express passes - leading engine LMS '5' No 44963 - and under the ash-disposal plant is an Ivatt '2' 2-6-0.
D. T. Flook

tol Bath Road shed. In May 1958, the 'Jubilees' allocated to the newly coded 82E were: 45572/7/45651/60/2/82/5/90/9.

All the Barrow Road 'Jubilees' are remembered as good engines. Their Class '6' rating in BR days meant that they were permitted to take 380 tons up the 1 in 80/69 of Fishponds bank, as against 345 for a '5', and 300 tons for a Compound. On the banks, however, the 'Black Fives' were considered the better engine, Barrow Road's 'Jubilees' being supplemented by '5s' on express passenger turns. Of these, Nos 4804/5/12/43 and 5272 were at the depot in November 1945, the first two having been allocated to Bristol when new. They were replaced by Class '5' variants equipped with Caprotti valve gear, Nos 44743-7. These engines were generally regarded as 'terrible' on the banks, and Trevor Glasspool also recalls their being 'slow to get going but went like the wind once they had got past Yate on a northbound train '.

The early postwar cross-country expresses offered passengers slow journeys. The 7.40am Bristol-Newcastle of November 1949 did not reach Sheffield Midland until 12noon - 166 miles in 4hr 20min. The train was booked to make its entry to Newcastle Central, at 2.58pm, after 7hr 18 minutes' travelling - at an average overall speed of 40mph. Southbound, the 8.10am Newcastle-Bristol reached Birmingham New St at 1.5pm - 205 miles in 4hr 55min - and arrived at Temple Meads for 3.20pm. The current Cross-Country Newcastle-Bristol High Speed Trains take $4^3/_4$-$5^1/_4$hr for the journey.

Both these expresses of 1949 were among the speedier trains on their route and, as with today's cross-country trains, they made a number of intermediate stops. The 8.10am called at Durham, Darlington, York, Rotherham Masborough, Sheffield Midland, Derby Midland, Cheltenham Spa Lansdown, Gloucester and Mangotsfield.

These pair of trains were chosen for an experimental operation during early May 1950. 'Jubilees' from Barrow Road

and Holbeck were tried out on through workings between Bristol and Newcastle. The Barrow Road engine worked from its home city, but the Holbeck engine was scheduled to work to Newcastle with a passenger train from Leeds at the start of the week, and to return similarly. The London Midland crews worked as far as York where they were relieved by Heaton men.

Starting on 1 May, Barrow Road's No 45682 *Trafalgar* worked to Newcastle with the 7.40am from Bristol, coming south the next day with the 8.10am from Newcastle. Holbeck's choice lasted for just one return trip and then failed. Its intended working with the 7.40am to Newcastle of 4 May was taken by Barrow Road's No 45690 which returned to Bristol the next day, and worked to Newcastle on 6 May. As

In low-key sunshine and a biting cold wind during January 1957, an identified 'Jubilee' forges up Ashley Hill bank out of Bristol with the northbound 'Devonian'. The northbound 'Devonian' took the ex-GWR route out of Bristol. Conversely, the northbound 'Cornishman' from Penzance-Wolverhampton was routed over the Midland route to Yate.
George Heiron

No 45682 had completed the trials without mishap, the exercise was a feather in the cap for the Bristol depot. Tom King remembers the trials well:

> Possibly it was found that the length of the through working led to steaming problems as the fire became clinkered. On each trip the tender was specially stacked with coal to the limits of the loading gauge, but fortunately there were no mishaps on that score. Some years later, a Barrow Road crew working back from Leeds with the southbound 'Devonian' learned that when passing through Defford station a piece of coal had shot off their 'Jubilee's' tender and had broken the ankle of someone standing on the platform.

These trials were conducted at a time when there was a concerted effort on BR to increase the length of through engine turns. It all depended on the preparation of the engines, the quality of coal supplied, and the crewing arrangements. It was a finely judged business. For Barrow Road the longest regular engine and men's working was a lodging turn from Bristol to Leeds, out with the northbound 'Devonian', back with the southbound train. Complaints from men who wanted to return to Bristol earlier in the day saw the engine and men's workings altered, and then the return was with the 7.40am Bradford Forster Square-Bristol. With the change in diagrams, the southbound 'Devonian' was worked by a Holbeck 'Jubilee' which returned north after a speedy turn-

(Opposite)
Smartly turned-out by its home shed, No 45662 Kempenfelt *emerges from the north portal of Wickwar Tunnel with the northbound 'Devonian' of the early 1950s. This was a lodging turn to Leeds for a Barrow Road crew, and they were scheduled to return south with the engine the following day. Note the reporting number 'M240'.*
George Heiron

(Below)
Returning home: in June 1953 No 45685 Barfleur *nears the summit of the climb to Rangeworthy, between Wickwar and Yate, with a Newcastle-Bristol express.*
George Heiron

(Opposite)
*Having brought in the southbound 'Devonian' one 1954 afternoon,
No 45572* Eire *is being 'disposed of' on its home shed, and stands
under the ash-disposal plant. In the background are Ivatt 2-6-2T
No 41243 and a '3F' 0-6-0T. Holbeck was known to 'borrow' a
Barrow Road engine from the northbound train for its own turn
with the southbound working.*

George Heiron

(Above)
*Careful supervision and hard work by shed staff enabled Barrow
Road's 'Jubilees' to be the 'talk of the line'. No 45682* Trafalgar,
*destined to be the last of its class on the shed's allocation, stands in
its home shed in 1960.*
*Nearby is '5' No 44825: by this time the shed did not have any of
this class on its allocation, only BR Standard '5s'. Note the
substantial and typical Midland shed buildings and, in the yard, the
gas lamp-standards with metal ladders attached.*

George Heiron

round with the same day's 7.20pm Bristol-Newcastle Mail.
    At 21 years of age, Dennis Moriarty was exceptionally
young for a fireman on a mileage turn, and from 1951 put in

a five-year stint on Barrow Road's working with the 'Devonian'. He comments:

> We went to Leeds three days in one week, twice the following
> week when we also worked on Sunday to Derby where we
> lodged. Bristol men worked alternately with Holbeck until that
> depot lost its share and then Barrow Road worked daily. It was
> hard work but I was lucky. My driver was Fred Barnett, a real
> gentleman who looked after his fireman. He worked the engine
> 'light' - others were 'heavy' with the regulator and cut-off. The
> old drivers knew exactly where they were 'on the road' by
> sounds and echoes from the track and structures. They had all
> the passing times off by heart.

Len Glasspool also put in his time as a fireman on the
mileage turns.

> In 1953, I fired on No 45690 *Leander*. But there was a notice-
> able difference with those 'Jubilees' paired with the small
> Fowler tenders, notably No 45561 *Saskatchewan*. These rode
> more roughly, and the engines running with them often had prob-
> lems with their injectors.

The routine when working the northbound 'Devonian' was for the crew to book on Barrow Road shed at 11am, where they prepared their own engine. Then, the 'Jubilee' ran tender-first to Temple Meads to await the arrival of the train behind a Western Region engine. With the higher degree of vacuum created by GWR-design engines, the strings had to be pulled on the coaches before the 'Jubilee' backed on. Away from Temple Meads at 12.30pm, unusually the train followed the former GWR route out of the city in order to call at Stapleton Road and then ran via Filton and Westerleigh West Jcts before joining the Midland line north.

Firemen endeavoured to prevent the engine emitting smoke or blowing off at Temple Meads which made it difficult to get the fire right for the engine to tackle the climb out of the city. At Gloucester Eastgate water was taken, and the boiler filled up, but often the tender tank was topped up during the Cheltenham stop to guard against the chance of empty water-troughs at Haselour, north of Tamworth.

At Bromsgrove, the train came to a stand to obtain bank-ing assistance up the Lickey incline. Two 0-6-0Ts were reckoned to be better than the famed ex-Midland 'Big Bertha' 0-10-0. In view of the slow speed up the bank, there was little risk of the train engine's fire being torn apart; if more effort was needed from the banking engines, the crew sounded the whistle.

After the ascent of the Lickey, the train called at Birmingham New St where the through coach (or two) from Bournemouth West to Sheffield was attached. This had come north on the 'Pines Express' and cooled its heels for 25min or so at New St awaiting the 'Devonian'. As the 'Devonian' continued north, water was taken at Derby and

Barrow Road's No 45682 Trafalgar *showed its mettle during the trials in 1950 with experimental through engine workings between Bristol and Newcastle. Damp, misty conditions add to the atmosphere as this 'Jubilee' heads through Yate in the mid-1950s with the 10.15am Bristol-Newcastle. Barrow Road men would work the 'Jubilee' to Derby. Beyond the barrow crossing is Yate South Jct, divergence of the spur to Westerleigh N Jct.*
D. T. Flook

Sheffield, sometimes even at Rotherham. By Derby, the 'Jubilee's' coal supply was usually running low and the remaining stock was brought forward in the tender. On this later stage of the run to Leeds, the four-mile climb at 1 in 100 to Bradway Tunnel represented hard work for engine and crew. Len Glasspool remembers one run when a 'Jubilee' loaded to 15 coaches entered Bradway Tunnel at no more than 15mph.

After the booked arrival at Leeds City at 6.13pm, the Barrow Road men worked the engine to Holbeck depot where it was coaled before going on to the ash-pit. The crew departed for their lodgings, having taken care to hide the long-handled shovel and other tools under the footplate - 'to prevent their being pinched'. After oiling round the next morning, the engine was ready to work home with the southbound 'Devonian', at 10.48am from Leeds City.

No 45651 Shovell *approaches Charfield with a Bristol Temple Meads-Bradford Forster Square express in August 1953.*
George Heiron

Len Glasspool recalls:

> I worked with Driver Harry Huntley and at Holbeck he always gave the tube-blower a shilling to blow through the tubes on our 'Jubilee'. It was always my job to prepare the engine, the driver spending his time talking to other footplatemen.

On the return run of the Leeds turn there was a risk that by Birmingham the fire might become 'dirty' and, if so, the fireman was unable to rectify matters in view of New St's city centre location. The restart from New St was difficult, up the 1 in 75/80 through the customarily damp tunnels. Care had to be taken to avoid 'catching the water'.

There were twelve men in the express passenger link, and also a spare link. Barrow Road had three lodging turns within the twelve turns in the EP link:

> Northbound 'Devonian' to Leeds City, lodge, back with the 7.40am Bradford Forster Square-Bristol the next day.
> 10.30am Bristol TM-Newcastle, to Derby, lodge, and return

with the next day's 2.10am Derby-Bristol parcels.

2.15pm Sundays Bristol-Leeds to Derby, lodge, return with the Monday 1.30am Derby-Bristol parcels.

Other turns included:

5pm Bristol TM-York to Birmingham NS, back with the 4.45pm Bradford FS-Bristol TM.

1.10am Bristol TM-Sheffield to Gloucester Eastgate, back with 7.10pm Newcastle-Bristol TM Mail.

The LMS favoured cyclic diagrams, a practice continued by the London Midland Region. Generally, this meant that the diagrams for a shed's enginemen and its locomotives did not coincide. For instance, the Barrow Road 'Jubilee' or '5' dia-

And here is a Barrow Road 'Jubilee' being 'borrowed' by Holbeck - on 4 June 1955, No 45699 Galatea *eases away from Trent station with a Glasgow St Enoch-St Pancras express.*
John P. Wilson

grammed to the 7.40am Bristol TM-Bradford FS express was crewed by Saltley men who had worked to Bristol overnight. At New St, they were relieved by another set of Saltley men who took the 7.40am to Sheffield.

At one stage, a Barrow Road engine worked by Derby men was used north of Derby and as far as York on the 7.40am Kings Norton-Newcastle express (the unusual starting-point was a consequence of the stock being stabled there overnight), engine and men returning to Derby with the 12.43pm Newcastle-Bristol. The Bristol 'Jubilee' then regained its home depot the following day with the 2.10am Derby-Bristol parcels, this time handled by a crew from its own shed. South of Birmingham, the 12.43pm from Newcastle was worked by Barrow Road men on a Derby Class '6' and sometimes they had to endure Derby's sole 'Patriot' No 45509 which was detested - 'worn out' was the kindest description. Incidentally, the 7.40am from Kings Norton was later worked to York by Bournville shed's solitary 'Black Five' which returned with the late afternoon return working to Birmingham New St.

To give some idea of the complexity of the enginemen's workings of the 1950s, at one stage the southbound 'Devonian' was worked between Leeds and Bristol by five sets of men: Millhouses (Sheffield) to Sheffield; Nottingham men to Derby; Derby men to New St; and Gloucester men who handed over the engine at Eastgate station to another set from their shed.

Enginemen of the time frequently complained of the deterioration in standards that often accompanied cyclic diagrams and the common-user working of engines. They criticised workings - such as that just described - which involved sets of men from different depots stepping on and off footplates. Railway operators retorted that such arrangements were essential to make the best use of locomotives and men. The recollection from Barrow Road is that the cyclic diagrams worked quite well, providing the booked engines were not purloined to cover other workings.

Len Glasspool recalls:

One day Holbeck swiped the 'Jubilee' we had brought from Bristol for one of its turns to St Pancras, and gave us a '5' in replacement. We struggled for steam all the way to Bristol and arrived 75min late. The foreman at Barrow Road said he would examine the '5', and soon found out why it had been swapped for the 'Jubilee' - its large tubes were well and truly blocked.

The Barrow Road 'Jubilees' were well-maintained, the result, say the enginemen, of the careful supervision and high standards of the mechanical foremen at the shed, particularly Bill Backhouse and his successor, Jack Davis. Bill is remembered as someone who 'led from the front'. literally so on those occasions when almost at a run he ducked under a 'Jubilee' under repair and brained himself in the process! When a crew booked a fault on the repair card, the shed's fitters attended to it promptly. Fitter Don Flook throws more light on the standards of Barrow Road's repair workshop :

I was privileged to work with Vernon Young whose abilities on the centre-lathe were the stuff of legend. Year in and year out, he provided meticulously machined axleboxes, eccentric straps, big-end brasses, bushes and the like to the finest of tolerances. In later years he became a supervisor at Bath Road depot. Vernon was ably supported by Percy Weekes who variously operated the planing and shaping machines, radial drill, wheel-lathe and overhead crane. As he was not apprentice-trained, despite his versatility he was not paid the top fitters' rate! The combination of these back-room boys and the shed fitters played no small part in the fine performance of the 'Jubilees' and Barrow Road's other engines, too. Other fitters that come to mind are Ted Farr, Bob Smallridge, Alec Read, Hughie Bannerman, Maurice 'Mick' Longden, Frank Norley and Bert Nettles.

Driver Tom King comments:

With the advent of Bill Blakesley as district locomotive superintendent, he was the force who had the 'Jubilees' cleaned and

polished. With Bill Backhouse as foreman, and some enthusiastic cleaners, the result was that the Barrow Road allocation was the talk of the line. Because they made their mark the result was that all received promotion!

Don Flook and Bob Dearnning well remember when No 45660 *Rooke* arrived back at Barrow Road after a general overhaul, the first of the shed's allocation to be painted in BR Brunswick green:

Bill Blakesley lined up the cleaning chargeman and his cleaners, and instructed them how the locomotive should be cleaned. No 45660 was turned out to royal engine standards for some time and used on the 'Devonian'. Bill also introduced the practice of picking out the backing of the 'Jubilees'' nameplates in red paint.

Dennis and Len remember:

All the fitters were excellent and knew their jobs. We remember Fred James, Charlie 'Chad' Chadwick, Walt Turner and Charlie 'Hawkeye' Harding. The boilersmith was Bill Hunt, and the boiler washer, Frank Laigh. All our passenger engines were examined every 24hr.

The locomotives were turned out really well - the shed staff spent hours on some of them. No 45577 *Bengal* was particularly good, and plenty of emery paper was used up burnishing its side-rods and buffers.

No 45577 was something of a favourite. M. Quirk, a cleaner and fireman at Barrow Road reckons that this engine and No 45682 *Trafalgar* were particularly good. The latter was used more than once on the annual weekend excursion from Bristol to Blackpool for the illuminations. C. W. Portch recalls the October 1960 working as faultless when this engine was worked throughout by Barrow Road men who lodged overnight at Blackpool. Len Glasspool was No 45682's driver, with Peter Easterbrook as his fireman, on the October 1963 Blackpool excursion which was probably the last to have been worked from Bristol with steam. John Childs remembers a Barrow Road 'Jubilee' being serviced on Bournville shed when working an excursion taking Bristolians to Cadbury's factory.

George Green was in the Divisional Operating Superintendent's Offices at Derby during the 1950s, and comments:

Besides being involved with engine and men's workings, I had ample scope to travel behind Midland Division 'Jubilees'. I was mainly acquainted with the Bristol stud, a depot noted for the cleanliness of its locomotives. I consider that 45690/9 were the two best at Barrow Road.

C. Abson was a fireman at Bournville, and in the 1950s this shed had a turn between Derby and Birmingham New St on the 4.45pm from Bradford Forster Square, regarded as the first southbound mail train of the evening. This train reached its journey's end at Bristol Temple Meads just after midnight.

> We used to have a Bristol 'Jubilee' and always found them a great pleasure to work on. Quite often we would have 13 or 14 coaches and vans behind us but these engines were a match for anything. No 45690 *Leander* was the best of the bunch. She used to ride like a coach and you could keep her on the mark all the way. We were relieved at New St by Barrow Rd men who were always glad to see their own engine.

In November 1958, Barrow Road received three 'Patriots', Nos 45504 *Royal Signals*, 45506 *The Royal Pioneer Corps* and 45519 *Lady Godiva*, their transfer reported in the railway press as intended to cover for the overhaul of the shed's 'Jubilees'. Locally it was believed they had arrived only for storage. At any rate, they do not appear to have been used much until mid-1959 but over the next couple of years put in a fair amount of work on the shed's Class 'A' turns. Despite the grisly reputation of Derby's No 45509, the Barrow Road trio were not regarded unfavourably once their firebars had been altered to provide wider spacing. In May/June 1957, the shed had lost its Caprotti '5s' in favour of BR '5s' which proved much more popular.

Once the control of Barrow Road had passed to the Western Region, much of the depot's old spirit was lost. The new owner was soon involved in planning the dieselisation of the Birmingham-Bristol services, and from July 1961 BR/Sulzer Type 4s took over many of the express workings, a process completed in theory, if not in practice, from the start of the 1961/2 winter timetable. The newcomers were serviced at Bath Road depot, emphasising that the writing was on the wall for Barrow Road.

Just to underline the new order of things, in the four-week period ending 7 October 1961 six of Barrow Road's 'Jubilees' - Nos 45572/7, 45651/60/2/99 - were transferred to Shrewsbury. The diesels' lack of reliability meant that Barrow Road looked to just three 'Jubilees', Nos 45682/5/90, and the three 'Patriots' to cover for failures, and its few remaining principal turns. The 'Patriots' were condemned in March 1962, but the 'Jubilees' soldiered on, being picked off one by one during 1964, the last to go being No 45682. Fate ensured that No 45690 was reunited in Woodhams scrapyard with former stable-mate No 45699.

During the early 1960s, Barrow Road saw an increasing number of ex-GWR engines, some coming for repair from further afield in the '82' district, and by 1965 only three or so of its allocation of 41 engines were not of GWR or BR design. With the expectation that Barrow Road would close, enginemen such as Len and Trevor Glasspool and Dennis Moriarty transferred to Bath Road and to diesels. By now the last steam shed in Bristol, Barrow Road had entered its twilight days, and closed in November 1965. The buildings were demolished during the early autumn of 1966.

The overbridge carrying Barrow Road across the site of the shed has also disappeared, and the locality's main landmarks nowadays comprise the St Philips Causeway - a motorway-style road - and a refuse collection point which dispatches bulk refuse trains to Appleford.

7

LIVING WITH THE ARISTOCRACY
of Neasden and its Pacifics

Featuring a London shed, surrounded by a purpose-built housing scheme, and with an often overloked allocation of Pacifics

The noise from the passing road traffic on the A406 North Circular Road is deafening, and across the road the flags of the Ikea furniture centre flap in the chilly breeze. Turning round, there seems something vaguely familiar about the pair of streets of terraced houses, and even more so about the turn of century semi-detached houses. In the foreground, there is an open space intended as a recreation area. Sadly, vandals have taken their toll and the space for seating is littered with rubbish. The street names of Woodheyes Road and Gresham Street at first sight have no obvious connotations, and behind them is a solid fuel depot and a modern industrial building. The railway bridge provides the only clue to the

(Previous page)
Neasden's 'A3s' seemed to be a little shy of the camera. Here the 34E shed-plate is worn by No 60050 Persimmon, *at the head of a Sunday afternoon Manchester London Road-Marylebone express on 9 July 1950, and seen passing Nottingham Goods signalbox, south of the River Trent bridge.
No 60050 was allocated to Neasden on 3 February 1949 (official transfer date), remaining there until 24 June 1956, apart from a sojourn at Kings Cross from July-October 1955.*
John P. Wilson/Rail Archive Stephenson

(Right)
Neasden shed in 1962, shortly before closure. By then, diesel multiple-units had taken over local services from Marylebone, and the shed's duties comprised main line work including the Marylebone-Nottingham semi-fast trains and a variety of special workings, some parcels trains and local freight trips.
London Borough of Brent

association of this area with the heyday of steam.

These streets of houses were built to provide homes for the families of the enginemen and other railwaymen who manned and maintained the locomotives and trains of the newly formed Great Central Railway. The terrace houses have more than a passing resemblance to the railway buildings on the rest of the GCR's London Extension. Their raison d'être is no more because 30 years ago the fuel depot took the place of Neasden locomotive shed.

Construction of the railway at Neasden began in earnest during 1897. South and east of Neasden's Dog Lane, and inside the semi-circular link which provided the GCR with access to the Midland's Cricklewood-Acton line, was constructed an engine-shed, capable of stabling 30 engines. More buildings rose north and west of Dog Lane, and these comprised a large carriage depot, much of which was spectacularly destroyed by fire in the early 1920s. The rebuilt structure was demolished by a flying bomb early in 1945 which also tragically wiped out a railway community centre with the loss of many lives.

To provide accommodation for the train crews and workshops staff and their families, as the new railway took shape an estate of 154 houses was built by the House & Shop Co on land leased from the GCR. The completed estate was then leased back to the railway which charged its tenants an all-in rent inclusive of rates and repairs. The principal street was

Woodheyes Road. In those days, it started at the revised line of Dog Lane, and was subsequently incorporated into Brentfield Road, nowadays better known as...the North Circular Road.

At the start of Woodheyes Road, on each side are four semi-detached houses, and these were intended for the managerial and supervisory staff who came from the Manchester offices of the Manchester Sheffield and Lincolnshire Railway, predecessor of the Great Central. Indeed, most of the inhabitants of Woodheyes Road and the adjoining Gresham Road had moved to Neasden from Manchester, Liverpool and Sheffield. There were, and apart from one or two replacements still remain, no less than 138 terraced houses in the estate which was completed by eight semi-detached houses known as Central Villas. Today these front the North Circular Road. The shed was reached by a footpath which spanned the canal feeder dividing it from the estate to its west.

This railway community was self-contained, and included

A smoky if impressive departure by Leicester Central shed's No 60052 Prince Palatine, *departing from Marylebone during 1949 with the down 6.15pm 'Master Cutler'. It is passing one of the 'N7' 0-6-2Ts allocated to Neasden at the time to work Marylebone-West Ruislip auto-trains. Note the carmine and cream painted late 1930s' LNER corridor stock, complementing the distinctive headboard carried by blue liveried No 60052.*
F. R. Hebron/Rail Archive Stephenson

a corrugated-iron school in Bridge Road which formed the southern exit from the estate. The local Co-op opened a shop in one of the semi-detached houses, and in 1910 a church was constructed in the triangle of land between Woodheyes and Gresham Streets; in 1924 it was re-erected on another site. Life on the railway estate, usually referred to as the 'Cottages', was semi-rural in those days, but became progressively less tranquil with the building of Wembley Stadium, and then the North Circular Road. There was good-natured rivalry between the Great Central men and those of the Metropolitan Railway whose own Neasden workshops and associated railway village were on the other side of the Met and GCR running lines.

Some of the original inhabitants remained in the estate's houses until comparatively recently, including John 'Old Timer' Dulson who had driven the first train to enter the new Marylebone station, and whose son was also an enginemen. Those living on the GCR estate remember the drivers of the pre-Grouping Marylebone-Manchester expresses as the 'Aristocracy', characterised as upright, hard-working and dignified men. 'Railwaymen bowed and scraped to the

driver and fireman of the down newspaper train', is one comment.

By the late 1930s, most of the enginemen associated with the early days had retired, just at the time that the former GCR express engines, the Atlantics and 'Directors', were being replaced on the Top Link jobs worked by Neasden shed. By the late spring of 1936, Gresley three-cylinder 'B17' 4-6-0s had been added to Neasden's allocation but the pre-Grouping locomotives, in particular the 'B3' 4-6-0s, were still to be found at work on the shed's duties. From September 1938, Gresley 'A1' Pacifics were drafted to GC Section sheds for the premier expresses, and in June 1939 the first came on Neasden's allocation. This process had the effect of displacing the 'B17s', and the Pacifics remained at work on the GC main line through most of World War 2.

In the immediate postwar period, the GC main line sheds received brand-new 'B1' 4-6-0s, and these were employed on the express trains. As business traffic recovered, so the loads of the expresses into/out of Marylebone increased, and the crews on the 'B1s' were hard pressed to maintain schedules. In the autumn of 1947, the 7.40am Sheffield-Marylebone and the 6.25pm return were named the 'Master Cutler'. The following autumn, the 10am Bradford Exchange-Marylebone and 4.50pm down became the 'South Yorkshireman'. Although running to slower schedules than those of the prewar expresses, the two named trains were faster -

(Opposite)
The second Gresley Pacific to be built was No 60102 Sir Frederick Banbury, *here in unkempt condition and allocated to Leicester shed. It is waiting at Nottingham Victoria with the 4.23pm southbound departure on 14 May 1951. To its left is No 60107* Royal Lancer, *transferred to Leicester on 4 June 1950 and associated with the GC main line until September 1957.*
T. G. Hepburn/Rail Archive Stephenson

(Below)
Flying Scotsman as No 60103 on the GC main line: at grips with a stretch of the ruling 1 in 176 gradient on the London Extension, this Leicester engine is working the up 'South Yorkshireman' near Lutterworth on 2 July 1952. Ahead are station stops at Rugby Central and Aylesbury.
T. G. Hepburn/Rail Archive Stephenson

and generally more punctual - than the corresponding Midland line trains to and from St Pancras, and so loaded well. When in good condition and competently handled, the 'B1s' were able to keep time, but frequently they were outclassed on the trains of ten or eleven coaches.

In February 1949, Pacifics returned to the GC main line. They were displaced from East Coast sheds as new Peppercorn 'A1s' entered traffic in quantity. Leicester acquired 'A3s' Nos 60048 *Doncaster*, 60049 *Galtee More*, 60053 *Sansovino*, 60054 *Prince of Wales*, 60061 *Pretty Polly*, 60090 *Grand Parade*, and Neasden, Nos 60050 *Persimmon*, 60051 *Blink Bonny* and 60111 *Enterprise*. By May 1949, Nos 60052 *Prince Palatine* and 60102 *Sir Frederick Banbury* were added to Leicester's allocation, in place of No 60053 which was transferred to Doncaster, and No 60090 which departed for Grantham. Now there were nine 'A3s' to handle the GC main line expresses but operation of the Pacifics was not without its constraints.

Although 70ft diameter turntables had been installed at Marylebone and Leicester stations before the prewar allocation of Pacifics to the GC, neither Leicester nor Neasden

(Opposite top)
Last view of a GC 'A3': transferred from Leicester on 15
September 1957, No 60106 Flying Fox *is seen two months earlier -*
on 5 July - waiting in No 3 bay platform at Leicester Central to
work the up 'South Yorkshireman'. In the other bay platform is
Neasden BR '5' No 73156, now in preservation.
T. G. Hepburn/Rail Archive Stephenson

(Opposite lower)
On 28 April 1956, No 60063 Isinglass *is still displaying a Kings*
Cross shed-plate a month after the 'A3' had been transferred to
Neasden. The scene is Leicester Central station and No 60063 is
working the lunchtime stopping train to Marylebone.
T. G. Hepburn/Rail Archive Stephenson

shed could turn these engines. They had to be turned at the respective stations before going on shed or, in the case of Neasden, were sent round the single-track loop which served Wembley Stadium station. Although Neasden and Leicester sheds had been well-equipped when built, they were not capable of carrying out heavier repairs on engines, particularly as they were unable to lift the 96-ton Pacifics. The general maintenance of these engines was the responsibility the main depot in each district, Kings Cross and Colwick respectively.

Whereas Neasden had enjoyed a fine reputation in prewar years, by the late 1940s maintenance standards were at a low ebb, and locomotive availability accordingly suffered. The late Bill Harvey has graphically described the problems he encountered at the shed when appointed shedmaster during this period. From 1937 the shed's allocation had been increased by a dozen or so engines as a result of the LNER assuming responsibility for providing motive power on all services over the Metropolitan & Great Central Joint line north of Rickmansworth. At Nationalisation, Neasden, by now coded 34E, was responsible for 75 engines. These covered main line duties, the suburban service from Marylebone to High Wycombe, local trains beyond Aylesbury routed via the Met & GC line, and workings from/to Rickmansworth on the London Transport Baker Street/City-Aylesbury trains.

Despite the prevailing difficulties, the Pacifics imparted prestige to the GC main line expresses. The 'Master Cutler' featured a distinctive headboard, and both this train and the 'South Yorkshireman' were allocated some of the best rolling stock available on the Eastern Region, including some of the later prewar coaches and the postwar steel-panelled stock. all in carmine and cream livery. The service of meals in the restaurant cars attracted favourable comment, and overall much remained of the enthusiasm and energy associated with the GCR and the early days of the London Extension.

The timetable current at November 1949 comprised the principal trains shown in Table 1. Although this timetable

---

TABLE 1

GC main line express passenger trains, as at November 1949

Down trains from Marylebone:

10.0am (via Met & GC Joint line and Aylesbury) to Manchester London Road arrive 3.29pm
12.15pm (via GW & GC Joint line and High Wycombe) to Manchester London Road arr 5.48pm
3.20pm (via Met & GC Joint line and Aylesbury) to Manchester London Road arr 8.55pm
4.50pm 'South Yorkshireman' (via Met & GC Joint line and Aylesbury) to Sheffield and Bradford Exchange arr 10.14pm
6.15pm 'Master Cutler' (via GW & GC Joint line and High Wycombe) to Sheffield Victoria arr 10.11pm
10pm Mail (via Met & GC Joint line and Aylesbury) to Manchester London Road arr 4.25am, and with through coaches and vans to Liverpool Central detached at Godley Junction

Up trains to Marylebone:

'The Mail', the 10.25pm ex-Manchester London Road (including through coaches at 9.30pm from Liverpool Central), routed via Aylesbury and arriving in Marylebone at 5.10am
7.40am from Sheffield Victoria, the 'Master Cutler' via High Wycombe, arriving at 11.25am
8.25am from Manchester London Road via Aylesbury, arriving at 1.58pm
10.0am 'South Yorkshireman' from Bradford Exchange via Aylesbury, arriving at 3.29pm
11.30am from Manchester London Road via Aylesbury, arriving at 4.28pm
3.46pm from Manchester London Road via Aylesbury, arriving at 9.34pm

Missing from this list as it was not a passenger train was the 1.45am newspaper train to Nottingham. This was the successor to the 2.32am paper train earlier mentioned and which ceased running in 1941.

marked a retreat from more ambitious timings introduced just two months earlier, the timings of the GC trains to and from Leicester and Nottingham compared favourably with the Midland main line expresses, but only the 'Master Cutler' was really competitive for journeys to Sheffield and the North. The punishing climb over Woodhead to Manchester contributed to the lengthy journey times of 5-6 hours for the 206 miles to/from Manchester. Some of the trains provided a valuable semi-fast service between the Midlands and South Yorkshire and the north-west, and the majority made a number of intermediate stops.

The 'South Yorkshireman' was the successor to through workings instituted by the GCR and Lancashire & Yorkshire

Railway in the early years of the century but its timings did not suit business travellers, and the passenger loadings of the up train were disappointing. Although the 'South Yorkshireman' was booked to load to ten or more coaches, by the early 1950s the remainder of the expresses seldom exceeded nine coaches.

Some changes occurred with Leicester's 1949 allocation of 'A3s' during the early 1950s, but until late 1953 Neasden's allocation of Nos 60050/1/111 was unchanged. For the most part, these engines were handled by enginemen in the shed's No 1 Link whose duties comprised the Down and Up Mails, the 10.0am express ex-Marylebone, and the Passenger Pilot at Marylebone station. The Neasden men worked one of the shed's Pacifics on the 10am down as far as Leicester, and usually returned with a 'B1' at the head of the 1.12pm Nottingham Victoria-Marylebone stopping train. They were relieved at Harrow on the Hill on this turn, as otherwise they would have been 'out of time' had they continued to Marylebone. The turn with the Down Mail took 'A3' and men to Leicester which was reached at 12.41am. There the Neasden

Upon transfer to the LMR's control in February 1958, Neasden shed was grouped under Cricklewood and received the shed-code, 14D. One of the new shed-plates is worn by 'V2' 2-6-2 No 60876, waiting at Marylebone with the down 'Master Cutler' in the last months that this named train ran on the GC.

T. G. Hepburn/Rail Archive Stephenson

engine gave way to one from the local shed and, after turning the 'A3' on the station's turntable, the crew awaited the 2.21am arrival of the Up Mail. On leaving Leicester the train was booked to load to 450 tons, and comprised three passenger coaches and no less than 19 vans containing lettermails, parcel-post, tobacco from Nottingham, and fish from Grimsby for London area stations.

Ron Dansie started his railway career at Neasden in February 1938, some of his earliest cleaning duties being on the 'Footballer' 'B17s' then on the shed's strength. He recalls his days as a fireman on the 'A3s' working the Down and Up Mails: 'The GC retained the practice of single-crewing on these turns and our engine was No 60051 *Blink Bonny*'. Comments Ron: 'If an engine was stopped for a boiler washout, then the crew were stopped, too. The older drivers were meticulous, and applied tallow to the wash-out plugs before they were refitted.' His driver was Albert Lane: 'His overalls were immaculate - and were as clean at the end of a week's work as at the start.'

Leicester engines and men covered express turns north and south of their home city. A typical turn with a Pacific involved working the Down Mail to Sheffield, returning with the up 'Master Cutler' to Leicester, then the 8.25am ex-Manchester London Road forward to Marylebone, to return with the 3.20pm down. The shed had No 60103 *Flying Scotsman* on its allocation in the early 1950s. Ron Dansie worked on this 'A3' a number of times but was not impressed with its mechanical condition which for a time restricted the engine to secondary turns including freight work. In their last couple of years on GC services at least, the 'A3s' were smartly turned out, and I well remember seeing them rumble across the bridge just south of South Hampstead station which carried the Great Central high above the North Western main line. A pleasant memory from earlier years is of the spectacle of Neasden's Nos 60050 and 60051 at the head of north and southbound expresses simultaneously passing my vantage-point at Wendover.

Neasden provided motive power for the cheap fare, guaranteed-seat 'Starlight Specials' operated on Fridays from 1953 until 1962 between Marylebone and Edinburgh (and later, St Pancras and Glasgow St Enoch). Although well-patronised, the discounted fares charged meant that the trains needed to be packed if they were to be profitable. In the 1950s, a Neasden engine, usually a Pacific, worked to Leicester whose shed provided one of its engines for the next stage to York, usually routed via Darnall, the Dearne Valley line, Mexborough West Junction and by way of the Swinton & Knottingley Joint line. From York, a fresh engine took over for the run along the East Coast main line to Newcastle, and then to Edinburgh. Neasden's No 60111 *Enterprise* worked the very first 'Starlight Special' out of Marylebone on 10 April 1953. These trains were frequently duplicated, sometimes even running in nine parts. Although a cafeteria car was provided for the first section of the train, Ron Dansie recalls occasions when trestle tables laden with food were set up at Leicester Central and other stations for nighttime

travellers on the duplicate 'Starlight Specials'.

A number of 'A3s' were swapped between GC section and GN sheds in the early 1950s, such that by the end of 1954 Neasden had a revised line-up of Nos 60050 *Persimmon*, 60063 *Isinglass*, 60108 *Gay Crusader* and 60111 *Enterprise*. Logs of runs published at the time indicated that, with the customary 300-ton loads, the 'A3s' had no difficulty keeping to, or bettering some of the sharp point to point timings. Without exceeding the line speed limit, 'even time', 60mph average runs were recorded between Aylesbury and Woodford Halse, for instance. When working the nine-coach 10am down, Neasden's No 60108 *Gay Crusader* was recorded by Ronald Nelson as taking no more than 29min 52sec for the 31.2 miles from Aylesbury to Woodford, with no higher maximum speed than 76mph. Those expresses running via Aylesbury frequently suffered severe signal checks between Harrow and Rickmansworth from preceding LT Metropolitan Line trains, while timekeeping was impeded by semi-permanent speed restrictions between Woodford Halse and Rugby, and north of Sheffield.

As in the case of No 60103 earlier mentioned, not all the Pacifics were in as good fettle as No 60108. One correspondent to the railway press said that the sight of an 'A3' at the head of an express 'made him fear considerably for the time of arrival at Marylebone or Leicester' and that the Pacifics were 'played out'. His outburst generated a sackful of fan-mail for the 'A3s', correspondents emphasising the fine work recorded with these engines between Sheffield and Manchester. This section of line was electrified in 1954, after which the Pacifics were denied the opportunity of showing their paces on the severe gradients up to Woodhead. Some speedy running was experienced north of Leicester, particularly on the sharp timing to Nottingham of the 'Master Cutler', and speeds in the mid-80s were noted.

The published logs reveal the diminishing size of the GC expresses. Whereas in the early 1950s, there are runs with fully laden 12-coach 'South Yorkshiremen', by the mid/late 1950s even the 'Master Cutler' had no more than 150 passengers on board. The late George Dow, an enthusiast for the GC if ever there was one, revealed in September 1959 the average number of passengers on each of the expresses between Marylebone and Sheffield was no more than 80.

The decline of the GC main line expresses owed much to the machinations of railway politics. In 1958, the London Midland Region gained control of the line, after expending some effort to improve services on the Midland main line. The GC line timetable of this period had changed little from that of 1949, except that the 11.30am from Manchester had been retired to a 2.10pm departure. The service on offer reflected the travel habits of prewar years and, with the exception of the 'Cutler', the Midland line had the more conveniently timed business trains.

In the lead-up to change of ownership, the Eastern Region reclaimed its Pacifics for GN line sheds, and the last departed from Leicester shed during September 1957. Neasden's final 'A3' was No 60108, transferred to Kings Cross on 27 January 1957. Immediate replacements for the 'A3s' were 'V2s' whose shorter length allowed them to be turned at Neasden shed. Many GC enginemen considered the 'V2s' were better suited to the route, and they ably demonstrated *Green Arrow's* capabilities during steam running from Marylebone in the late 1980s.

The departure of the Pacifics signified the death-knell for the GC line's express services. Generally the 'V2s' held the fort, aided by 'B1s', but LMS and BR Class '5s' made their appearance following the LMR's takeover of the GC main line. As forecast in the London Midland Region's Passenger Plan of 1959, the GC line's London expresses ran for the last time on 2 January 1960, and were replaced by a service of semi-fast trains between Marylebone and Nottingham.

Next came the closure of Neasden shed, on 18 June 1962. With its demise, Neasden's enginemen were dispersed. Some went to Marylebone diesel depot, but others, like Ron Dansie, stayed with steam, transferring first to Cricklewood during the period that this depot worked GC line turns, from June to October 1962, and then moving to Willesden shed when it assumed responsibility for the remaining GC turns.

An echo of the 1950s' GC Top Link motive power came

in the late 1980s during operation of the Sunday luncheon trains from Marylebone to Stratford-upon-Avon, and former Neasden enginemen demonstrated their expertise with the Gresley Big Engines. In the meantime, the railway estate comprising Woodheyes and Gresham Roads was designated a conservation area, and Marylebone station, by now reprieved from closure, was modernised, and its services revolutionised with the introduction of the Network Turbo units.

Finale: the 'Master Cutler' name was transferred to the Eastern Region's diesel-worked Pullman between Kings Cross and Sheffield, and here is the last southbound GC 'Master Cutler', waiting to leave Nottingham Victoria on 13 September 1958. The engine is Leicester 'V2' No 60842. The original intention was to withdraw the GC line's 7.50am ex-Sheffield and 6.18pm from this date, but they were retained until January 1960, the former down 'Cutler' being retimed in November 1959 to leave London at 7.15pm.
T. G. Hepburn/Rail Archive Stephenson

8

'FEET UP, DON, IT'S TRING'

Edge Hill shed and the Stanier Pacifics

One of the oldest and most evocative names in railway operation is Edge Hill, Liverpool which survived as a steam MPD until 1968. Now to recall the days of Stanier Pacifics on the 'Merseyside Express', and the terrors of the 'Scots' working the 9am to Leeds...

A gloomy winter Sunday in the late 1940s is already becoming dusk, a process hastened by the pall of smoke being emitted from Edge Hill shed by 100 engines whose fires have already been lit up in readiness for Monday's turns. The locality is dominated by railway facilities which sprawl for some distance but the skyline's most prominent feature is the parish church of St Mary's. Houses are clustered around the railway installations, mostly in terraced rows known as 'The Dales', and occupied principally by railwaymen's families. Certainly, most of the enginemen live close to the shed for they have to be within range of the knocker-up. On their way to book on for the 4pm shift, the young cleaners make their way to the shed, aptly described in a contemporary

publication as being 'in a maze of railway lines, east of Edge Hill station'.

Another form of transport announces its presence for the area is served by the Wavertree group of tram routes operated by Liverpool Corporation although buses will take over during the autumn of 1949. From Edge Hill station the approach to the shed is along Tunnel Road, into Wavertree Road, passing to Picton Road, until just past a railway overbridge, then turn left into Tiverton Street from where a cinder path leads through an uninviting tunnel under running lines to the shed. It is an inauspicious approach to one of the larger motive power depots, but not untypical for although they contribute smoke and grime to the neighbourhood, and plenty of noise into the bargain, such hives of activity seldom have triumphant entrances. After all, the railway is their main business, and many are effectively land-locked. The noise and dirt generated by the shed face stiff competition from Edge Hill's famed 'Grid-Iron' marshalling yard which is shunted by engines from the local shed.

Two of the young cleaners are Alan Corfield and Don Buckley. At this time, there are no less than six different cleaning shifts in each 24 hours at Edge Hill, each with 30 men. Having stowed their coats and belongings in the dor-

(Previous page)
Perhaps Edge Hill's premier turn in the No 1 passenger link began with the shed's engine and men working the up 'Merseyside Express'. Sporting the shed's black beret headwear, the fireman of 'Princess Royal' No 46207 Princess Arthur of Connaught *takes a break from his labours as the 'Merseyside Express' makes the most of level track north of Blisworth on 10 March 1956.*
D. M. C. Hepburne-Scott/Rail Archive Stephenson

(Above)
A 1952 view of the south-west end of the shed, showing the ill-fated rebuilt No 46202 Princess Anne *surrounded by local engines, including a '7P' 4-6-0 alongside, ex-LNWR 0-8-0 No 49355, and a pair of '3F' 0-6-0Ts - Nos 47487 in the distance and 47385 nearest. The girder bridge carries the connecting goods 'Circular' line from the 'grid-iron' reception sidings towards Edge Hill station and Wapping while the northern boundary of the shed behind No 47487 overlooks the line to Manchester which runs alongside at a lower level.*
Eric Treacy/Millbrook House Collection

(Opposite)
A Lime Street 'Chopper', ex-LNWR 'Coal Tank' No 58887, poses outside the south-western end of the shed, with the shed's unrebuilt 'Royal Scot No 46164 The Artists' Rifleman *on the adjoining road.*
H. C. Casserley

mitory, the cleaners fall-in, military fashion, ten in a row, three rows deep, ready for an inspection by the foreman cleaner. Then the shift will be split into working groups, with a hierarchy of tasks working from tender wheels to boiler. Engine cleaners not only experienced the usual pranks but more malicious practices, such as being incarcerated in engine fireboxes, or buried up to the neck in sand. Passed cleaners could be used for firing duties, and if not booked would often be in the Magnet cinema nearby.

Having moved up the ladder, typically Don finds himself with two other cleaners, given the task of cleaning the boiler of 'Princess' No 6206. That is preferable to a night working underneath the motion of an engine, working only by the light of flares which burn a mixture of paraffin and rape oil. All around is pitch-dark for the smoke from the engines has blackened the shed's electric lights and at best they emit an ineffectual glow.

Having set the scene, it is worth quoting one of the steam text-books which comments, 'it is during this engine-cleaning period that the foundation of the future driver's career is laid.' The younger men concentrated on cleaning parts of the engines, but the older cleaners assisted the fitters as they went about their tasks. Working underneath the engine was preparation for being a fireman when the driver expected his mate to 'do underneath', oiling the bogies, big-ends, little-ends and valves. So the cleaner did most of the fitter's work, attending to the wicks and trimmings and the corks plugging the syphon tops. On, say, the 8pm Sunday shift a fitter and

cleaner would be expected to prepare eight locomotives – four small ones, four large ones. Other tasks included assisting with putting in brick arches, no matter that the firebox was still distinctly warm.

Such duties are preferable to the task facing the steam-raisers. Working with their overalls tied at wrists and ankles, theirs is the job of lighting-up the engines' fires, and by the end of the turn their faces are uniformly black. As lighting-up progresses, smoke billows around the footplates and fills the shed, and contributions from numerous engines mean that by the early hours of Monday morning the inside of the shed will be enveloped in an evil, greenish and sulphurous fog.

If the preparation of engines is bad enough, then the disposing turn is arguably worse. Every eight-hour shift as many as 40 engines will come on shed for servicing and coaling. Usually bereft of goggles or gloves, the men emptying the smokeboxes, and dropping or raking-out fires are exposed to choking fumes and curtains of dust and ash. There were two foreman in charge of all this activity, an outside foreman in charge of engines in the yard, and the coaling stage, and an inside foreman who controlled the allocation of engines to turns and the chalking-up of the engine allocation board.

Viewed fifty years later, many will wonder why young men persevered with working conditions like this. Alan comments, 'we all did it with a will - different times, different people. Sometimes you wonder though, did it really happen?'

A cleaner's aspiration was to be a driver in the Top Link whose double-home jobs to London brought lucrative mileage payments. The rest of the attraction lay in the job itself. As a fireman in the Extra Link, recalls Don, a driver might turn to you, and say, 'you get hold of her - let's see how you shape'. 'Sitting in the driver's seat of a 'Princess' hauling the fourteen coaches of an Euston-bound express - it was a moment of bloody glory, a real adventure.'

Progression from cleaning to driving was rightly regarded 'as a long, and many times thorny path to the rising fireman or cleaner' as the authors of the *Locomotive Management* textbook put it. One of the Edge Hill drivers was Jack Perkins who was the youngest driver to join the Edge Hill No 1 Link - at the age of 50. The usual experience was fifteen years cleaning, fifteen years as a fireman, with eventual promotion to driver a matter of filling dead men's shoes.

Alan and Don were among the youngest passed firemen at Edge Hill after 16/17 or so years' service. Don was a little older in age but, in the railway's reckoning, younger in seniority. The number of wiring trains operated in connection with the Crewe-Liverpool 25 kV electrification meant

that firemen were automatically marked up. Says Don: 'The old drivers commented "here are you young fireman, going where angels fear to tread"...' That is some guide to the realities of being an engineman at Edge Hill, or many another steam MPD but the progression from cleaner to driver could be faster, as at Bushbury, for instance - or even slower.

Edge Hill's history as a railway centre dates back to 1830 and the opening of the Liverpool & Manchester Railway. Originally Edge Hill was the western limit of locomotive

(Opposite)
With the typical Edge Hill streetscape in the background, LMS '3F' 0-6-0T No 47519 poses near the arch taking the so-called Circular goods line over the shed area.
Eric Treacy/Millbrook House Collection

(Below)
The Edge Hill coaling stage in all its grimy glory in the mid-1950s. Patricroft 'Jubilee' No 45558 Manitoba *is standing on the 'column line', with a Stanier 2-6-4T behind. In the background are the sharply curved and treacherous Downhill carriage sidings.*
Eric Treacy/National Railway Museum

The entrance to Edge Hill MPD in July 1965, with the by now closed 'lodge' which is adorned with the entrance sign. Edge Hill No 11 signalbox is in the background.
Dennis Flood

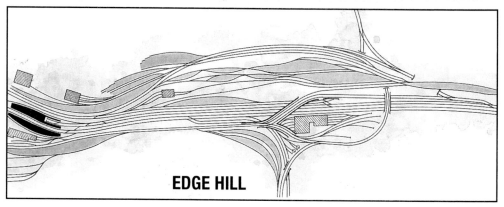

EDGE HILL

(Opposite top)
A begrimed Turbomotive No 46202 has come off the 'column line'
on 18 April 1950 while overhead the elevated line taking wagons to
the coaling stage curves round to meet the 'circular' goods line.
H. C. Casserley

(Opposite lower)
A late 1940s' shot with unrebuilt 'Scot' No 46164 The Artists'
Rifleman *approaching Bushey troughs at the head of a down*
Liverpool express which includes two of the new all-steel LMS
corridor composite coaches.
C. R. L. Coles

(Above)
No 46201 Princess Elizabeth *was on Edge Hill's allocation in the*
early 1950s, and in lined black livery passes Harrow & Wealdstone
station with an up Liverpool express.
C. R. L. Coles

working on the L&M, as stationary engines there worked
passenger trains by rope into their terminus at Crown Street,
and goods trains were hauled up the incline from the goods
station at Wapping. Lime Street station was not opened until
1836. Edge Hill developed as pivotal to Liverpool's railway
system. It was the junction for branches into the city's docks,
and the location of the major marshalling yard whose
inclined planes and pattern of sidings earned it the name of

the 'Grid-Iron'. At one time or another, the locality boasted
the widest imaginable set of railway installations including
the locomotive works of the Grand Junction Railway, goods
warehouses, coal yards, the extensive Downhill carriage sidings, and of course the locomotive shed.

Edge Hill shed occupied a cramped site, enclosed by running lines and freight yards, as depicted in the accompanying diagram. The shed building consisted of an original
structure and the so-called New Shed with 12 roads. All told,
there were 18 numbered roads to the shed (lowest number
on the north side), and No 19 was reserved for the shed's
breakdown train. Overshadowing these buildings were the
water tank fed by the River Alt, the accompanying water-
softening plant and, at least until the late 1930s, the tall chimney of the blacksmith's forge. One of the shed's specialities
was a hydraulically-operated wheel-drop. Once main line
diesel locomotives were allocated to Edge Hill, a two-road
repair shop was made available for the newcomers, fashioned
from the six highest-numbered shed roads. Diesels in traffic had to rub shoulders with steam but No 5 road was set
aside for them.

The shed site was bounded by the former L&MR line to
Manchester on the north side - but at a lower level - and, to
the south, sidings and the double-track goods lines looping
round from the 'Grid-Iron' in the direction of Edge Hill station. Entrance and exit from the shed sidings were by means

of a sharp incline at 1 in 27, this line being controlled by Edge Hill No 11 signalbox, but movements off shed to Lime Street came under No 4 box. The alternative to the gradient was to proceed to the shed via Rathbone Road sidings, but the 2-6-4Ts in particular tended to pick up their wheels and slide out of control.

Located between the elevated goods loop and the 1864 main line to Mossley Hill and Speke Junction was the remarkable elevated coaling-stage, built largely from concrete in 1913/4, in replacement of an earlier coaling shed. Wagons shunted up the ramp discharged their coal into a back-to-back array of electrically operated bunkers, three to each side of the stage. These coaled engines, those on one side discharging to the siding known as the 'Coal Hole', the remainder, fed with the top-grade coal for engines working the London turns, served the 'Column Line' from which a siding led to the turntable. Engines passing to the shed from the coaling-stage went through an arch beneath the goods loop.

Coded 8A by the LMS in 1935, Edge Hill was the main depot for a district that included the sheds at Warrington Dallam, Speke Junction and Widnes. Edge Hill's locomotive allocation numbered 136 in 1938, and 154 by February 1946. By then, the most numerous classes comprised the Stanier '5' 4-6-0s (31), ex-LNWR 0-8-0s (19), ex-LNWR 0-8-4Ts (13) used for shunting the 'Grid-Iron', 'Royal Scot' 4-6-0s (11) and, the pride of the shed, three 'Princess Royals' - Nos 6200/3/5. Pacifics had first come on Edge Hill's allocation during 1939 although one was allocated temporarily to the shed in 1936. Not to be overlooked were the nine 'Lime Street Choppers' at the shed, a type more prosaically described as ex-LNWR 'Coal Tank' 0-6-2Ts.

By 1950, Edge Hill's allocation totalled 112, including 13

(Below)
The Edge Hill men working 'Royal Scot' No 46152 The King's Dragoon Guardsman *will not have been pleased at the absence of the booked Pacific for the down 'Merseyside Express', seen passing Carpenders Park in the mid-1950s. There was a shortage of Pacifics at Edge Hill in early 1954, and again in 1957.*
C. R. L. Coles

(Opposite)
One long-serving Edge Hill 'Scot' was No 46124 London Scottish *here getting into its stride past Wembley Central with a Euston-Liverpool express of the early 1950s.*
C. R. L. Coles

'Scots' (Nos 46106/11/23-5/34/5/7/8/44/53/6/64), four 'Princess Royals' (Nos 46200/1/3/5), nine 'Jubilees' (Nos 45567/613/23/37/70/3/81/721/37), five 'Patriots', and 22 '5s'. Immediately before dieselisation of the London turns in 1959, the tally of Pacifics was seven - Nos 46200/3/4/7-9/11 - and out of an allocation of 124 engines there were ten 'Scots' - Nos 46114/9/23/4/32/42/7/55/6/64 - 11 'Jubilees' and 13 'Patriots'.

Following the dieselisation of the London trains, as from January 1961 the Liverpool-Newcastle service was similarly turned over to haulage by 'English Electric' Type 4 haulage. As a prelude to electric haulage to and from Crewe of cross-country services serving Liverpool, crew training with 25kV ac electric locomotives began early in 1961 on the Crewe-Liverpool line. As for Edge Hill's Class '8' power, although there had been intermittent allocations of 'Duchesses' during the mid-1950s, No 46233 was transferred to 8A in September 1960, followed by Nos 46229/41/3 during March 1961. By then, there were no regular turns for Class '8'

engines from the shed, and early in 1961 Edge Hill stored 'Princesses' Nos 46204/8.

The unreliability of the main line diesels ensured that the four 'Duchesses' working from 8A were employed from time to time on regular and relief Euston-Liverpool expresses, as well as on the West Coast main line, and hauling van trains and some fitted freights. By mid-1961, Edge Hill's only booked principal turns for steam involved two 'Royal Scots' working alternately on the Liverpool Lime St-Glasgow Central and return sleeping car expresses. The shed's Class '6' engines also featured on passenger turns to Birmingham, Chester and Holyhead.

Electrified working was inaugurated between Crewe and Liverpool as from 1962 although London expresses continued to be diesel or steam hauled for a couple of years. As late as a summer Saturday in July 1962, for instance, the down 'Red Rose' was hauled by Crewe North 'Duchess' No 46225 while the 2.5pm Euston-Liverpool was worked by 'Princess' No 46209. As the depot lost steam work, enginemen like

The handsome lines of No 46208 Princess Helena Victoria *are seen to advantage as the engine takes the down 'Merseyside Express' along between Bushey and Watford, with a beret-wearing driver at the cab window. Edge Hill's 'Princesses' were stored during 1961. The last on the shed's allocation was No 46208, withdrawn in October 1962.*
C. R. L. Coles

Alan and Don transferred to sheds such as Birkenhead Mollington St. In 1965 8A's steam allocation had shrunk to no more than 50 engines, comprising 26 '5s', 17 '8Fs' and seven '3F' 0-6-0Ts, and by January 1967 to 43, by which time 8A operated '5s' and '8Fs' only. Edge Hill lost its steam allocation on and from 6 May 1968, and early the next year much of the shed was demolished. The last steam working booked to Edge Hill shed took place early in the morning of 5 May 1968 when '5' No 44877 hauled empty stock out of Lime Street station.

To return to the 1950s and the days of Top Link steam working at Edge Hill, the main passenger turns were on the Euston expresses, and the Liverpool-Leeds/Newcastle/Hull service, on which the engines and men worked as far as Leeds City. In all, there were five passenger links, of which No 1 comprised the premier London and Leeds turns, No 2, also London and Leeds, No 3, turns to/from Crewe, and the remainder involved workings to Manchester, Bolton and Wigan North Western. Of the passenger links, Nos 1 and 2

were mileage turns, as was No 1 goods link which included the Camden and Carlisle fitted freight workings. On the mileage turns, extra payment was credited on the basis of every 15 miles over 140 miles' driving counting as 1 hour's extra pay.

There were about a dozen sets of men in each link. From No 1 goods link, a fireman would progress to No 1 passenger link. The London turns were all 'double-home', lodging turns and involved preparing the engine at Edge Hill, 3-3½hr running time to Euston, and taking the engine up the bank to Camden shed where the crew remained with it until it had been turned.

The most prestigious turn in No 1 Link found the crew setting out from Lime St at 10.10am on the 'Merseyside Express' with one of the 8A Pacifics, with the booked arrival at Euston being 1.45pm. In cases such as this where the crew were off-duty for 12 hours, they were regarded as having commenced duty at 1.30am the next morning and were paid accordingly. In fact, they booked on at Camden at 6am, in order to work the 7.55am Euston-Liverpool with a Camden engine, and accordingly received a 12-hour mileage payment. Drivers on contract mileage turns started their week by taking an express to Euston on the Sunday, then worked to London and back twice in the week, and on their rest day worked to Leeds and back. As Don Buckley comments: 'A driver working this turn was well and truly in the money.'

Until 1950, the Liverpool Riverside branch was banned to large engines, and the Euston boat trains were usually hauled by a pair of 'Lime Street Choppers' to and from Edge Hill station where they gave way to a 'Jubilee' or 'Patriot'. After the swing bridge over Princes Dock had been rammed by a ship, the opportunity was taken to replace it by a stronger structure, with the result that from March 1950 engines up to Class '6' were allowed to work into Riverside station, and the Euston boat trains now became an eight-hour through turn for a set of Edge Hill men. These were the days of numerous special and relief trains and, to cover such workings as well as the absences of regular men for holidays and sickness, the shed's Extra Link comprised no less than 52 sets of drivers and fireman.

As to the Top Link passenger turns during the 1950s, Edge Hill engine and men's workings to and from London did not necessarily correspond. One of the men's workings covered the up midnight sleeping car express to Euston with an 8A 'Scot', but they returned that evening with the 6.10pm down 'Merseyside Express' working their shed's 'Princess' which had come south on the 8.10am from Lime Street. Another turn began with the 9.50pm Liverpool-Euston which was diagrammed for an 8A 'Princess', the men returning from Euston with the 4.45pm down 'Shamrock' with the 8A 'Scot' off the previous day's 4.10pm Lime Street-Euston. Then there was the turn covering the up 'Merseyside Express', the men returning the next day with the Camden 'Duchess' working the 7.55am to Liverpool. Lastly, a turn began with the 4.10pm Liverpool-Euston which was one of the slower expresses and called at Crewe, Stafford, Nuneaton, Rugby and Watford Junction. These men returned as far as Crewe with the next day's 1.35pm Euston-Perth. The 4.10pm up was a turn for an Edge Hill 'Royal Scot', and accordingly (and literally) this was regarded by the enginemen as a 'rough job'.

During the 1950s there were at least three and up to eight 'Princesses' based at Edge Hill. If at least three were available they covered the depot's trio of turns booked for Class '8' engines. One Pacific came to London with the 8.10am from Lime Street, and returned with the 6.10pm down 'Merseyside Express'. The second working was with the up

'Merseyside Express', the engine heading north the next morning with the 12.10am down sleeper to Lime Street. If a third Pacific was to hand, it was employed on the 9.50pm Liverpool-Euston parcels, and the next day's down 'Red Rose'. At 5.25pm from Lime Street, the up 'Red Rose' was the return working for the Camden 'Duchess' off down 7.55am 'breakfast flyer' from Euston-Liverpool/Manchester, both among the fastest trains on the London Midland Region. Earlier this turn had been frequently worked by No 6202, the Turbomotive. It was regarded by Don as, 'some loco - no one knew what its potential was - it was only worked with two nozzles open out of the six available for the forward turbine.'

The Edge Hill 'Royal Scots' had three diagrams to and from London. Apart from the 4.10pm up, after which the engine returned home with the next day's down 'Shamrock', a second working brought one of the class to London on the midnight sleeper from Lime Street (another well-remembered 'rough job') to return with the 2.30pm Euston-Liverpool. The final turn was on the 2.10pm Liverpool-Euston whose engine returned home in stages, beginning with an Euston-Bletchley slow train, and from there to Crewe on a parcels train. During the summer the Euston-Liverpool service was expanded, notably by the 10.30am Euston-Liverpool which carried the 'Manxman' headboard, also affixed in summer to the year-round 2.10pm up.

The significance of this last title was that the trains served as connections for sailings to and from the Isle of Man while the 'Shamrock' was the advertised service for the overnight ships to and from both Belfast and Dublin. In all cases, passengers made their own way between the Liverpool waterfront and Lime Street station, as only the boat trains serving the Canadian Pacific, Cunard and Elder Dempster liners ran to Riverside station. The up and down 'Merseyside Expresses' conveyed a through portion to and from Southport Chapel Street, attached at Lime St but detached at Edge Hill station. The Liverpool-Euston expresses were some of the heaviest on the London Midland Region. They loaded to 13, 14 or 15 coaches for most of the week, but on Fridays or for special traffic 16-coach trains were not unusual.

Both Alan Corfield and Don Buckley had their share of firing the two classes of LMS Pacific on the Euston-Liverpool expresses. Alan comments:

> With both types, apart from careful preparation before the run, the secret was to keep the back corners of the grate filled up, having placed a big firebrick in each corner of the grate at the footplate end. At any one time, there was probably something like three tons of coal in the firebox. You fired steady and often, but on a 'Duchess' the fireman would not have kept up if he had fired as the 'textbook' had it, in '6s and 8s': six shovelfuls, then eight shovelfuls! It was a matter of physically pushing the coal into the left and right-hand corners of the firebox. You kept the area just behind the firedoor well banked up with coal, to ensure that the heat coming through the door flap was minimal. If not, the blinding heat was such that it was impossible to fire. Generally, you ran with the dampers kept shut or

almost so.

In both directions the start to the journey was uphill. The climb out of Euston up Camden bank could pull the fire about, even with the tankie pushing at the back of the train. If you didn't repair the fire by the time you had passed Willesden there was no chance to get it right afterwards during the steady climb up to Tring. Detailed knowledge of the road was vital,

as this enabled you to adjust the rate of firing to the gradients, and allowed you to let the water level in the boiler drop when approaching a booked stop, or when picking-up water on the troughs.

When it came to managing the boiler, as with most engines the water level rose falsely in the gauge-glass when the regulator was opened, and with a Pacific you had to be careful not

'Duchess' Pacifics were allocated to Edge Hill for short periods until
a longer-lasting allocation came from 1960/1, by which time diesels
had taken over the regular London turns. One of the short-term
lodgers at 8A was No 46255 City of Hereford, here approaching the
platform ends at Watford Junction with a lengthy up 'Shamrock' of
the late 1950s.
Photomatic 4606/RAS

The 'Princesses' and 'Duchesses' required almost identical
handling although it's safe to say that the 'Duchesses' were
freer steaming and rode more smoothly. Quite simply they
were magnificent machines, and about the only criticism I had
was that the safety valves projected back into the cab roof and
you tended to get your share of steam and water! The
'Princesses' were the more tricky of the two, particularly when
they were becoming due for a boiler washout.

These Pacifics regularly worked the down 'Merseyside
Express' which until 1959 was booked to take 3hr 40min for
the 193¾ miles to Lime Street, having run non-stop to Mossley Hill. At first sight, the train did not appear to be tightly
timed, but it was. In any case, you were running just 5 minutes behind the 'Mancunian' and you played steam with the
Longsight men at Euston to ensure that they didn't delay you.
Coming down the bank into Crewe, you looked into the tender and saw a wall of coal. That was when you wished for a
'Duchess' with the coal-pusher in the tender. We called them
the 'second fireman'.

The restart from Mossley Hill was up a stretch of 1 in 113.
By this stage, the fireman was naturally running down the fire,
as well as being mentally and physically exhausted - he had no
reserves to call upon. When off-duty I frequently used to lis-
ten out for the down 'Merseyside' making this difficult start,
and when I was firing on this turn my family came along to see
us get away. Just a few minutes later, the train made its unad-
vertised stop at Edge Hill where the Southport portion was
detached. That was difficult, too! The train ran through the
station in order to clear the points at the south end of the station, to allow the 'tankie' working to Southport to come on to
the back of the train. Until the time when a repeater signal was
fitted to the tunnel wall, the fireman had been obliged to walk
back to get the right-away, and the crew then did their best to
run the train smartly down the bank into Lime Street.

Alan was mentioned 'in dispatches' on one occasion in 1954
when he was fireman on the 7.55am Euston-
Liverpool/Manchester and unaware that a train-timer was
aboard. The log of this exceptional run has been quoted in
most of the published works on the 'Duchesses'. Later
named the 'Lancastrian', from the summer timetable of 1954
the 7.55 down was booked to take no more than 136 minutes
for the 140.6 miles between Watford Junction and Crewe, at
an average speed of 62.5mph, the journey times from Euston
to Liverpool and Manchester alike being scheduled to take
just 3½ hours. On the run in question, Alan was in the Spare
Link and replacing the regular fireman to Driver Bert 'The
Mad Major' Aitchison who, in Alan's words, was known 'for

to risk uncovering the firebox crown, as some crews found to
their cost. Firemen had their own ideas as to working on either
the live or the exhaust steam injector; some relied on the live
steam injector - on the driver's side - and worked the exhaust
injector on the minimum setting. Others applied the reverse
approach, and only used only the live steam injector in an
emergency.

trotting them along'. With No 46229 *Duchess of Hamilton* at the head of 16 coaches for 535 tons gross, the minimum speed maintained on the climb to Tring was 64mph, and the net time Watford Junction-Crewe was reckoned as just 125$^1/_4$ minutes.

Don Buckley also fired on the 7.55am down, and recalls:

> You could call the king your uncle when you were firing a 'Duchess' on that train. It was something as you swept through the suburban stations, and the crowds waiting the suburban trains to London turned to watch you! Mind you, you shovelled hard all the time from Watford up to Tring! You didn't shut the firedoor, just put the flap-door up. You fired round the firebox to a rhythm, and were as light on your feet as if dancing in a ballroom. I never remember steaming problems with a Pacific working this train. You built up a tremendous fire before departing from Euston, and maintained the water 'halfway up' the gauge-glass. You tried hard to avoid blowing-off! Once clear of the station, you kept the water level 'three parts up in the glass', and the heat from the fire was unbelievable. I always worked on the exhaust steam injector, and used the live steam injector only in an emergency, or if I needed to top up the boiler. Regulation dress for an Edge Hill fireman was a black beret, scarf round the neck and the regulation 'slop'.

Once up trains had passed Tring summit, the almost continuous downgrades to Euston ensured that high speeds were reached, even with just a breath of steam passing to the cylinders. Even with the regulator shut, Don Buckley remembers that speeds of 90mph were attained with a 'Duchess' on the descent from Tring. One published run featuring a 'Princess Royal' at the head of a 490-ton express shows that an average speed of 81.8mph had been maintained over the 47 miles between Castlethorpe and Wembley. On his retirement from BR, Don was presented with a shovel inscribed, 'Feet up, Don, it's Tring', hence the title for this chapter. He recalls: 'It was a wonderful feeling once you were over the top at Tring. Looking over the cabside there was just a silver blur from the engine's coupling rods.'

Despite the prestige of the London turns, Edge Hill men regarded some of the other workings from the depot as equally exacting or as more physically exhausting. Don Buckley comments:

> The Leeds road was definitely harder. Men in the No 1 Link working to Leeds on 'Royal Scots' or rebuilt 'Patriots' had bruises as big as your hand from being flung about the footplate as the engine rounded the curves between Stalybridge and Leeds. The firemen probably knew the road better than the driver as the majority of signals were sighted on that side. You never put the shovel down all the way up to Diggle, in either direction. At least on the London road there was usually the chance of a 5min 'breather'. We worked out to Leeds on the 5pm Liverpool-Newcastle, with a Farnley Junction LMS '5' as pilot from Manchester Victoria, and returned with a stopping train which made 28 stops to Liverpool. You were soaked to the skin with sweat after working this turn, and after booking-off spent the time getting coal-dust and smuts out of your eyes. Even after a wash, you looked just like Dusty Springfield!

An Edge Hill 'Scot' or 'Patriot' worked out on the 9am Lime St-Newcastle, to arrive in Leeds City at 11.13am. Here the crew turned their engine by hand on the station turntable and brought forward the coal in the tender, before departure at 1.5pm with the 9.55am Newcastle-Liverpool. The pairing of Class '7s' on the 9.55am ex-Newcastle was frequent, the pilot being a Longsight engine which had worked over the Pennines and on to York with the previous night's 10.40pm Liverpool Mail.

Other well-remembered Edge Hill duties included working with ex-LNWR 'Super Ds' through the steeply graded tunnels to and from Wapping, downhill when the guard was controlling the train by means of one of the eight-wheeled 'tunnel brakes', and uphill with the driver giving the engine the gun. Then there was the afternoon Tue Brook-Carlisle fitted freight routed via Ormskirk to Preston where the train was turned out in the wake of the 'Caledonian', and green lights were the order all the way. On one memorable occasion the driver decided to risk Shap unaided - and Don and the '5' did their stuff. Come 1964, and Alan and Don departed for Birkenhead Mollington St shed, with the opportunity to become drivers and to work '9Fs' at the head of the Bidston-Shotton iron ore trains. Don Buckley was the driver of '5' No 44690 on 5 March 1967 when this engine worked the last Birkenhead-Paddington service train.

Today, you need to be in the know to find any evidence of Edge Hill shed - and nothing more is left than some of the trackwork. The surrounding area is now home to what the marketing men call a technology park - but was it ever different in the steam age?

9

'WHEN I START, DIG IN!'
Old Oak Common's
Top Link work

Old Oak Common was the largest locomotive shed on the Great Western Railway, and on the Western Region, and by any standards a remarkable establishment in terms of size, locomotive allocation, and the duties handled by its enginemen and shed staff alike

On a summer Saturday in the 1950s, Old Oak Common depot worked at something like the limits of its abilities. During the morning, the pressure was on to turn out engines and enginemen to work holiday trains to the West, South and West Wales, and Cambrian Coast. From early afternoon, and into the evening, the emphasis switched to disposing of the numerous engines released from trains bringing homecoming holidaymakers to Paddington. Everything at Old Oak Common had to be squared up during that crucial 2-10pm turn on the Saturday, and during the course of Sunday morning so that the depot was ready to start the new week in reasonable shape.

On typical 1950s' peak Saturdays, no less than 20 scheduled expresses for West Country destinations including Weymouth were booked to leave Paddington between 7am and noon. Yet these represented no more than a third of the main line expresses despatched from Paddington's main line platforms during the busiest seven-hour period from 9.15am. On average, there was a departure every 6min or

(Previous page)
'Smoke and ash were everywhere...' well describes this atmospheric
scene of the fire-pits at Old Oak Common and the southern,
'passenger-side' of the coaling-stage. Note the mountains of ash and
the travelling steam grab-crane. Facing the cameraman is 'Hall' No
4976 Warfield Hall.
Rail Archive Stephenson/Photomatic N805

(Above)
Granted that the outside of the shed was none too glamorous, but the
interiors of the four roundhouses provided a memorable sight. This
scene of one of the roundhouses dates from just prewar days and
indicates that the engine cleaning of old was not all it was cracked
up to be!
C. R. L. Coles

so. Very often, relief trains were also put on and, even on a peak Saturday, there might be excursions to Newbury Racecourse as well.

Such intensive working put Old Oak Common as a whole at the heart of the operation. The locomotive shed had to provide engines and men for the empty stock sent to Paddington to form outgoing trains, and main line power for the subsequent departures. For the scheduled summer Saturday morning departures, just under 50 engines were usually required, 20 more than for the scheduled weekday service. Anything up to 350 coaches had to be conjured up from Old Oak Common's carriage sidings, or worked in from other stabling-points. The majority of engines were turned out from Old Oak Common which could draw on

nearly 60 Class '7' and '8' engines of its own allocation. Also, Southall and Reading depots were called upon to supply engines and men to cover some of the trains, and their empty stock workings. A lesser proportion of engines and carriages was provided from trains arriving at Paddington, and whose engines were turned and serviced at the nearby Ranelagh Bridge yard, located alongside Royal Oak station.

Of course, Old Oak Common was involved in more than express train and empty stock working, and the summer Saturdays or other peak days such as before Bank Holiday weekends were untypical of its usual operations. Such occasions called on Old Oak Common's resources and strengths, and it was seldom found wanting.

It may have dominated its immediate locality, but Old Oak Common was just one in a necklace of major railway installations in London's north-west suburbs. The others comprised the Underground Group's Acton Works, the locomotive depot, carriage sidings and yards at Willesden Junction, the former Great Central locomotive depot and yard at Neasden, itself just a stone's throw from the Metropolitan Railway's works and depot and, to the east, the Midland Railway's locomotive depot and carriage sidings at Cricklewood and the nearby Brent freight yards. There was railway housing at Neasden, and in later years the GWR had provided the Acton Garden Village estate for Old Oak's enginemen and their families.

Of the motive power depots serving the London passenger termini north of the river, Old Oak was unusual in dating from the 20th century. Most of the capital's other locomotive depots were much older, and consequently a muddle or awkward to work - or both. In common with the Great Central's shed at Neasden, Old Oak was purpose-built, but on a much larger scale. Located three miles from Paddington, Old Oak had been built in replacement of the historic but outdated and constricted locomotive depot at Westbourne Park, no more than $1^1/_4$ miles outside the terminus.

That said, Old Oak did not cater for all the GWR's engine servicing needs in the London area. Southall shed was more important in providing motive power for westbound freight trains, and for handling incoming engines from trains terminating at Acton yards. As earlier mentioned, the locomotive yard at Ranelagh Bridge also fulfilled a crucial role.

Old Oak Common was completed in March 1906, the largest of a series of depots to be built by the GWR over the ensuing 20 years, in which the depot's layout followed the 'internal turntable' principle by which the main building's interior featured one or more turntables with radiating roads. This type of layout made it easier to get engines in and out of the shed without having to move dead engines. Old Oak was the largest of its type, with four 65ft turnta-

---

TABLE 1
Old Oak Common's allocation of Class '5', '7' and '8' passenger and mixed traffic engines as at 5 October 1957

'Kings'

6000 *King George V*	6012 *King Edward IV*	6019 *King Henry V*
6002 *King William IV*	6013 *King Henry VIII*	6022 *King Edward III*
6003 *King George IV*	6015 *King Richard III*	6023 *King Edward II*
6007 *King William II*	6016 *King Edward V*	6024 *King Edward I*
6009 *King Charles II*	6018 *King Henry VI*	6028 *King George VI*

'Castles'

4082 *Windsor Castle*	5034 *Corfe Castle*	5065 *Newport Castle*
4089 *Donnington Castle*	5035 *Coity Castle*	5066 *Sir Felix Pole*
4090 *Dorchester Castle*	5038 *Morlais Castle*	5074 *Hampden*
4091 *Dudley Castle*	5040 *Stokesay Castle*	5082 *Swordfish*
5001 *Llandovery Castle*	5043 *Earl of Mount Edgcumbe*	5084 *Reading Abbey*
5006 *Tregenna Castle*	5044 *Earl of Dunraven*	5087 *Tintern Abbey*
5007 *Rougemont Castle*	5052 *Earl of Radnor*	5092 *Tresco Abbey*
5008 *Raglan Castle*	5055 *Earl of Eldon*	5093 *Upton Castle*
5014 *Goodrich Castle*	5056 *Earl of Powis*	5099 *Compton Castle*
5029 *Nunney Castle*	5060 *Earl of Berkeley*	
7001 *Sir James Milne*	7017 *G.J. Churchward*	7030 *Cranbrook Castle*
7004 *Eastnor Castle*	7020 *Gloucester Castle*	7032 *Denbigh Castle*
7008 *Swansea Castle*	7024 *Powis Castle*	7033 *Hartlebury Castle*
7010 *Avondale Castle*	7025 *Sudeley Castle*	7036 *Taunton Castle*
7013 *Bristol Castle*	7027 *Thornbury Castle*	

'Halls'

4900 *Saint Martin*	5932 *Haydon Hall*	5945 *Leckhampton Hall*
4919 *Donnington Hall*	5936 *Oakley Hall*	5954 *Faendre Hall*
4925 *Eynsham Hall*	5939 *Tangley Hall*	5987 *Brocket Hall*
4977 *Watcombe Hall*	5940 *Whitbourne Hall*	
5931 *Hatherley Hall*	5941 *Camption Hall*	

'Modified Halls'

6959 *Peatling Hall*	6978 *Haroldstone Hall*	
6961 *Stedham Hall*	6990 *Witherslack Hall*	
6962 *Soughton Hall*	7902 *Eaton Mascot Hall*	
6973 *Bricklehampton Hall*	7903 *Foremarke Hall*	
6974 *Bryngwyn Hall*	7904 *Fountains Hall*	

'47xx'

4700   4701   4702   4704   4708

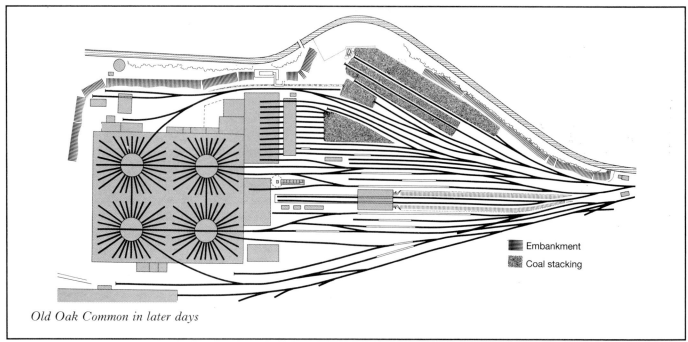

Embankment

Coal stacking

Old Oak Common in later days

(Opposite)
At first sight, this does not look like the entrance to one of the roundhouses but Old Oak's No 5044 Earl of Dunraven *(mentioned in the text) was easing back into the pair of roundhouses nearest the lifting shop - or 'Factory' - which appears to the right of the picture. Note that the entrance to the left of the picture is more utilitarian. This is because it was added later to ease access problems.*
R. C. Riley

(Below)
A 1958 picture at the shed of Fireman Ted Abear (to the right) with Driver Arthur 'Barney' Evans alongside Old Oak Common's No 7010 Avondale Castle, *prior to working to Swansea with the 6.55pm Paddington-Fishguard. On this double-home job, engine and men would return with the next day's 1.30pm from Swansea which was the forward working of the 11.10am ex-Milford Haven. Ted comments: 'From Newport we were fast to Paddington, arr 5.50pm. The load would be 10 vehicles and with a good loco and a clear run you could arrive 10min early.'*
Ted Abear

BR shed listing.

To the south side of the main building was a huge coaling-stage, surmounted by a water tank with capacity for 290,000 gallons. Loaded coal wagons were propelled up a pair of elevated tracks to deliver fuel which on each shift was shovelled into trolleys by a team of six coalmen. The trolleys were pushed to four double and two single tips, from where the coalmen tipped the contents into the tenders or bunkers of waiting engines. Express passenger engines were supplied with the best South Wales coal, and (generally) used the south side of the stage; tank and goods engines, the north side. Typically, a 'King' needed 10-12 tubs to fill the tender. In contrast to the other 'Big Four' companies, the GWR made no use of mechanical coaling-plants because its CMEs distrusted the reliability of these facilities, and also held the view that the traditional coaling-stage facilitated the mixing of the various grades of coal supplied.

Access to the shed was controlled by the Engine Shed signalbox. Incoming engines were segregated into express passenger, and other ranks, and accordingly progressed to the appropriate side of the coaling-stage. A running foreman was on 'outside' duty in the area of the coaling-stage and fire-pits, and reported the numbers of engines coming on shed to his counterpart 'inside' who allocated them to the next booked job. Suitable workings were found for 'unbalanced' engines - meaning those without a booked turn.

After coaling, the engines' smokeboxes were emptied, and their fires cleaned, and they were watered before being stabled inside the shed. The fire-pit roads were on each side of the coaling-stage, the labourers' tasks being somewhat eased in later days by the provision of travelling

bles, each with 28 roads, surrounded by a massive red-brick building measuring 444ft by 360ft.

Adjoining the eastern wall of this structure, and served by a traverser, was the Lifting and Repair Shop. This featured a 30ton overhead crane in the main shop, as well as a wheel-lathe, and associated fitters', smiths', coppersmiths' and carpenters' and machine shops. Extensive use was made of electricity at Old Oak for the operation of turntables, and for lighting and machinery, the power being supplied by the generating station provided for the electrified Hammersmith & City line.

The Lifting and Repair Shop at Old Oak had been intended to relieve Swindon of some of its workload of intermediate repairs to locomotives, but such activity ceased during the early 1930s although the 'Factory' retained some repair work thereafter. Nearby were extensive offices, including the headquarters of the London division locomotive superintendent. Old Oak was accordingly the principal depot in the Division, and became 81A in the

A September 1957 picture of 'Castle' No 5082 Swordfish *taking water in course of being prepared to work the 3.30pm Paddington-Penzance. This was a double-home turn to Plymouth for No 5082 and its crew, Driver H. Keen and Fireman Ted Abear.*
Ted Abear

grab-cranes. During World War 2, shelters had been erected around the pits, the intention being to shield the glare from engine fires.

Conditions at Old Oak Common rapidly deteriorated during the 2-10pm shift on summer Saturdays. Ted Abear was a fireman at Old Oak from 1954, and became a driver in 1962. He vividly describes the situation:

> Smoke and ash were everywhere. The passenger and freight-side fire-pits would be chock-full of engines, all of which would have to be pulled out low in steam, or dead, on the Sunday morning, to be made ready for the next day. The fire-droppers had to place burning oily waste on the engines' brick-arches to be able to see when raking out the fires. Remember that none of the GWR engines had rocker-grates, and the fires had to be cleaned through the fire-hole! The fire-droppers were on a bonus rate over and above their normal quota of engines to be attended to. Passenger engines might end up on the freight side of the stage, and 'Kings' and 'Castles' sometimes received a tender of 'eggs' (ovoids).

Old Oak men seldom failed to take advantage of better quality coal elsewhere, as Ted Abear recalls. 'Landore shed was known for its Oakdale coal, and on the double-home jobs to Swansea we did our best to fill up there. This excellent fuel opened up like a cauliflower as it burnt'. One of the London shed's problems was its hard water and to combat this Afloc water treatment was introduced in the 1959/60 period, as Ted describes. 'Solid brown tablets were used, and placed in a mesh trap located in a hole cut in the top of an engine's tender tank. The water in the tank looked dirty when the tablets dissolved, and the foaming that resulted was liable to cause priming. When the locomotives with Afloc water treatment went for boiler washout, a muddy solution poured out'.

Old Oak Common shed was a big place. Back in 1906 it had provided employment for nearly 800 men, almost two-thirds of whom were drivers, firemen and cleaners. Having described the buildings, facilities, and problems - what about the enginemen and their rosters? There were 12 Links, of which Nos 1-4 were the Top Links, with 12 turns - a week's work - in each. No 5 Link which had 48 turns was popularly known as the 'Washing-machine and telly links',

'I ain't...having No 6973...' said Driver Bill Church. Well, here is Bricklehampton Hall *being prepared at Old Oak during 1958. Old Oak's 'Modified Halls' were used on some of the residential trains, the famed 5.35pm Oxford-Paddington, the less important Class 'I' workings, and for summer holiday trains.*
Ted Abear

the term giving some clue to its earning-power.

Much of Old Oak's work was relatively unchanging from year to year, such as the local freight and yard trip workings, and the empty coaching stock and West London line turns. There were more changes to the express passenger turns, in line with the alterations to the passenger timetable. 'When the proposed alterations to the timetable were made known, often that changed the work available to Old Oak, and hence the locomotive diagrams and enginemen's Links. The Local Departmental Committee sat in on it all,

Surrounded by piles of smokebox char, 'King' No 6022 King Edward III *stands on the passenger-side fire-pits in the summer of 1958, having worked in on the 7am Weston-super-Mare-Paddington. By the winter 1960/1 timetable, nearly all the Paddington-Bristol expresses had been dieselised.*

Ted Abear

Passenger engines were serviced on the 'freight-side' of the coaling-stage at Old Oak, usually at peak periods, but here is No 3440 City of Truro *at this location, having worked into Paddington with a morning peak-hour train in 1957. This was not long after the engine had been returned to traffic at Didcot shed.*

Ted Abear

although with few firemen on the LDC it was the drivers who had the say', says Ted Abear.

The system of Links meant that it took 15 years or so for a fireman to reach the Top Link then, having passed as driver, another 15 years to regain the top. Old Oak had its 'Top Eight' system by which, on the periodical retirement of a batch of drivers, the top eight Passed Fireman became

drivers, and everyone else moved up a Link. Ted Abear comments:

In 1954, eight Southall men - including me - transferred into No 6 Link, consequently blocking off promotion for Old Oak men in No 7 Link. There were some comments, as you might expect! The drivers said, 'you blokes from Southall are all the same - you keep the footplate clean, better than some of the Old Oak firemen'. My dad was a driver at Southall and always told me, 'the footplate is your home for 8 hours, you need to be as clean and tidy as possible'.

Some of Old Oak Common's senior drivers were celebrities on, and off, the railway. There was J. W. 'Jim' Street, an engineman at Old Oak (and had started at Westbourne Park) from 1891 until 1936. He was renowned as the driver of the prewar 'Cheltenham Flyer' for some of the train's fastest trips. Walter Harris was a driver at Old Oak from 1925 until the late 1950s, and had driven for the Royal Engineers at Salonika during World War 1. Harry 'Rommel' Jermey was always recognisable by his goggles, hence the affectionate nickname. Ted Abear's father had fired to him on double-home turns to Severn Tunnel with a Dean Goods, and Ted was Harry's fireman on his last driving turn. Stan Newton was driver, and Ted Abear the fireman, when Peter Handford brought his sound-recording equipment on to the footplate of a 'King' working the down 'Inter-City'. Bert Potter was known as the 'Royal Train driver', and had been chosen for various test specials. He was quoted as saying, 'do as much as you can, as quick as you can'. With Stan French as his fireman, Bert Potter was reliably recorded as achieving 108mph with 'King' No 6015 in 1955 when this engine was first fitted with a double chimney. Enginemen talked of Potter 'going for it', and some said that 115mph was the maximum speed. Some of the old drivers enjoyed fiercesome reputations, such as Charlie Brown who was popularly regarded as a man who 'broke the fireman's back, and lifted bridges with the engine's exhaust'. He told Ted Abear who fired to him once, 'not to believe everything you hear.'

As elsewhere, there were occasions when Old Oak lost work to other depots. Ted again:

After some dispute with management over double-home turns, Old Oak lost some of their work to/from Swansea. To keep the enginemen's route knowledge to Swansea, we were left with one turn in No 2 Link, Saturdays excepted, working the 6.55pm Paddington-Fishguard Harbour, to return from Swansea with next day's 11.10am Milford Haven-Paddington. Also, we worked the Fridays only 8.55pm Paddington-Milford, and the next day's up 'Pembroke Coast Express'. My mate was Driver Arthur 'Barney' Evans, an excellent engineman, and a good mate to work with.

Old Oak Common enginemen's route knowledge was extensive but, as elsewhere, it had to be maintained. If a driver had not been over a route for three or six months, he would have to have a 'refresher'. Old Oak men worked to Plymouth and Swansea on double-home (lodging) turns (in summer, also to Newton Abbot), and more widely over the Western main lines on out and home workings: to Bristol, via Bath and via Badminton; to Gloucester; to Wolverhampton and Shrewsbury; to Cardiff via the Severn Tunnel, and via Gloucester. There was just a single turn on the Worcester line, as far only as Kingham. In South Wales, most Old Oak men had signed for the Vale of Glamorgan line from Barry through to Bridgend, a route frequently used for the weekend diversions of Paddington expresses, and also over the Swansea District lines. Many also had route knowledge to Cheltenham via Barnwood, so that Old Oak could cover the working of specials between Paddington and Cheltenham Racecourse.

Special workings featured largely in Old Oak Common's engine and men's workings. Spare men booked on every

hour, and the roster clerk had the first call on them. If due to book on, say, at noon for a special working, they would be called upon to report at 10am. Ted Abear:

> Every day the roster clerks at the shed received their Special Train Notices, and the turns would be set out on the boards in the signing-in room. These included, for instance, work-

(Below)
During the 1950s, Old Oak Common turned out some of the smartest engines in London such as 'Castle' No 7017 G. J. Churchward, on shed on 29 August 1959. By contrast, the home shed's No 5040 Stokesay Castle *standing on the fire-pits in the background is noticeably work-stained!*
R. C. Riley

(Opposite)
Before its acceleration in 1954, the 'Bristolian' was by no means a flyer. Here is the train of the early 1950s, arriving at Bath Spa behind Old Oak 'Castle' No 7032 Denbigh Castle. *Reporting No 119 applied to the train's pre-1954 departure-time from Paddington of 9.5am.*
D. T. Flook

ing empty wagons for broccoli traffic to Taunton where we would be relieved, to return with a loaded train. On race meeting days, there were four special trains between Paddington and Newbury Racecourse. Then the chief London running inspector, Dick Pettifer would ask the locomotive crews, 'Who wants to go to the races?' In the Racecourse station sidings two or three firemen would look after the engines. On a dry, sunny day some of the enginemen would sit up on the engines' tenders to watch the races while others would stay in the train reading rules and regulations, or taking a nap.

Such special workings declined fast in the early 1960s, yet as late as January 1962 Old Oak turned out three 'Kings', Nos 6009/15/27, to work specials to Plymouth for an FA Cup-Tie match between Spurs and the local team. The following month, four 'Kings' and three 'Castles' powered similar Footex excursions from Paddington to the

Hawthorns Halt which served West Bromwich Albion's ground. By then, there was no longer the customary annual outing for an Old Oak 'Castle' to Birkenhead Woodside at the head of the Grand National special from Paddington. As with many of Old Oak's special turns this working was allocated the depot's best 'Castle' of the moment. In 1957, for instance, No 5035 *Coity Castle* was the choice for the special, the engine having worked to Cheltenham Racecourse with the royal train a fortnight earlier. For royal duties the engine would be taken out of service a week beforehand to be prepared, and it would be made steam-tight.

During the 1950s, the Western Region's London Division had an extensive programme of excursion trains to race meeting and football matches, and summertime ADEX (Advertised Day EXcursions) trains to seaside resorts. Ted Abear recalls these turns as providing good days out for the families of enginemen and guards. 'We would work the

(Above)
As from the summer 1954 timetable, the 'Bristolian' ran to a 105-minute non-stop schedule to Bristol, as well as being allocated a set of GWR-design Hawksworth coaches. Over the ensuing year the train was 'King'-hauled, as recorded in this study of Old Oak's No 6024 King Edward I at speed, passing Corsham and its goods shed. From summer 1954 the down 'Bristolian' carried the reporting number of '116'.
D. T. Flook

(Opposite)
By 18 July 1956, the date of this photograph, the 'Cornish Riviera Limited' had regained something of its former style, what with the handsome engine headboard and distinctive carriage roofboards which adorned the chocolate and cream painted set of coaches. The up train is headed by Old Oak's double-chimneyed No 6015 King Richard III which is seen pulling away from Newton Abbot. From the winter 1956/7 timetable the up train was worked by a Laira 'King'.
R. C. Riley

train from Paddington with a 'Castle', stopping to pick up passengers at suburban stations. The destinations varied but included Barry Island (in which case we would be relieved at Cardiff) or Weston-super-Mare (Locking Road excursion station). Our wives would bring a change of clothes for us. We would wash and change on the train, and then spend the day on the beach with the family before working the train back in the evening.'

On summer Saturdays, some of the usual weekday trains were triplicated, such as the 'Royal Duchy', the 1.30pm from Paddington. Its group of trains generally provided the sight of a '47xx' 2-8-0 at the head of the 1.25pm to Kingswear, although from 1958 onwards the '47' was switched instead to the named train. Ted Abear remembers one such firing turn on the 1.25pm, working with Driver Jack Batterbee on No 4704. They were relieved at Taunton and returned with a holiday train from Paignton.

The 'Duchy' had a D800 diesel and its driver, Bob Smitheram, told Jack that he would catch him up by Read-

ing. Jack got the '47' going, also goaded by the signalman at Southcote Junction waving a duster from the window. Despite its eight-coupled wheels, the engine rode well, and down past Lavington I became alarmed at a loud booming noise - woom, woom, woom - from the cab roof - it sounded like something being played by Rolf Harris. Noticing my concern, Jack merely commented, 'That happens with these engines at 80mph.' Officially, they were restricted to 60mph. We gave the D800 driver an appropriate sign when he passed us at Taunton!

Ted worked on '47s' on an Old Oak turn which took them to Bristol Temple Meads with the 'King' booked to the 6.30pm Paddington-Bristol-Plymouth, the crew returning with a '47' on the 'Cocoa' fitted freight from Bristol East Depot to Paddington via Westbury. He remembers the big 2-8-0s as economical on coal and water, and distinctive for their pole reversers.

Old Oak Common engines and men covered some of the GWR and Western Region's most prestigious workings. On the West of England route, Laira and Old Oak 'Kings' and men shared double-home turns. In the winter 1956/7 timetable, for instance, Old Oak's engines had three turns: the down 'Cornish Riviera Express', returning from Plymouth with the 6.20pm Penzance-Southall milk train; the 1.30pm 'Royal Duchy', the engine returning at the head of the 8.45pm Penzance-Paddington sleeping car train; and the 9.30am Paddington-Plymouth, back with the 3.45pm Penzance-Paddington perishables. There were three similar diagrams for the Laira 'Kings'. Old Oak shared the working of the 'Torbay Express' with Newton Abbot shed. During the currency of the winter 1958/9 timetable, the two classes of 'Warship' diesel-hydraulics largely displaced steam from the Plymouth workings although until 1962 'Kings' continued to work to Plymouth on summer trains.

Ted Abear recalls:

I was in the Plymouth Link during 1961. You could go for weeks without working on steam - unless you were unlucky. Once we went down to Plymouth with D814, and expected to

return with it the next morning on the 8.30am up 'Mayflower' to Paddington. When we got to the shed, we were told that D814 had been taken to cover the 7.15am from Plymouth whose booked 'Warship' had failed. We looked at the duty board but no engine was shown for the 8.30am. We were told that double-chimneyed No 5098 *Clifford Castle* had worked down from Bristol on a fitted freight and was being prepared for us although it needed a 'bit of work'. No 5098 looked as if it was falling apart. We had a rough trip to Paddington and arrived 45min late, having cleared the tender of coal and with me, the driver and Inspector Bill Thomas working hard for 225 miles.

Most of the Paddington-Bristol express workings were shared with Bath Road shed, and Old Oak men covered the down 'Bristolian', and the 9.5, 11.15am, 1.15 and 6.30pm down. In the summer 1954 timetable, in both directions the 'Bristolian' was accelerated to a 105min non-stop schedule. At first, the service was worked by an Old Oak 'King' out and back, Old Oak men in charge of the down train, and a Bath Road crew working to Paddington. By September 1955, the train was being regularly worked by a 'Castle', and before long the diagram was changed so that the 'Castle' off the down train returned to London with the noon express from Bristol. The up working was then covered by a Bath Road engine which returned home with the 8.5pm from Paddington.

Old Oak's usual choice of 'Castles' at the time included Nos 5034/56, 7001/32. Ted recalls some of the exploits with the down 'Bristolian': 'It went out of Paddington like a rocket, and the fireman got stuck in straight away. Usually, the driver eased back the cut-off to 15% once the train was well on the move, and sometimes down to 12$\frac{1}{2}$%. At Didcot, I remember that the waiting bowler-hat brigade avoided boarding their train to Paddington until the 'Bris-

tolian' had come through. Once, when Driver Bill White was working a "King" he really had their heads turning. The engine's front bogie was rocking as it tore through Didcot East Junction, and the "King" passed us so fast that its side-rods were a-blur, something I only saw on one other occasion'.

Other expresses on the Bristol road were almost as fast. One was the 1.15pm down, booked in 96$\frac{1}{2}$min for the 107 miles to Bath Spa. When this accelerated timing was introduced in 1954, the train was worked by Bath Road shed but, as from the winter 1958/9 timetable, it passed to Old Oak, and the engine returned on the 4.15pm from Temple Meads. Once the 1.15pm down had got going, Driver Tommy Worth's technique was to open the regulator wide, and to drive 'on the screw'. This train, says Ted, 'had to get going, and was always allocated one of Old Oak's "good 'uns", such as No 5027 *Farleigh Castle*'.

Another fast Bristol line working was short-lived, and was known to Old Oak men as the 'Afternoon Bristolian'. This was the 3.5pm from Paddington which reached Bristol Temple Meads in 130min via Badminton, and its Special Load timings included a 75min booking to a first stop at Swindon. The return working to Paddington was at 6.10pm and took 125min overall. Both trains were introduced in the summer 1957 timetable but lasted only until the economy cuts introduced in late June 1958. One day when Ted was spare, he was fireman to Bill Church who was a driver in No 1 Link.

Bill saw that the 3.5pm was booked to have 'Modified Hall' No 6973 *Bricklehampton Hall*. 'I ain't bloody having that engine', he said, and stormed into the foreman's office. 'Change the engine, the wheels are too small for this job, Sixty-nine Seventy-three won't do it!' Bill and Foreman George Coles were slanging each other, and questions of birthright were raised. George gave in and said, 'take Fifty Forty-four and get off the shed!' No 5044 was *Earl of Dunraven*. Once we were at Paddington Bill told me, 'When I start, dig in! We are booked first stop Swindon in 75 minutes.' I must have dug in to his satisfaction because when we stopped at Swindon Bill turned to me and said, 'What do you think of these fast trains? You've done very well'.

Such fast trains were undoubtedly more expensive to run. 'Digging-in' meant that a lot more coal was burnt. Swindon's calculation were that in normal running a double-chimney 'Castle' might burn 36lb coal per mile, but that 44lb/mile was more likely for the limited load trains such as the 1.15 and 3.5pm ex-Paddington.

As from the summer 1959 timetable, the 'Bristolian' became a turn for a 'Warship' diesel, as did the 11.45am from Bristol. More workings were dieselised in winter 1960/1 timetable. By 1962, steam had lost express turns over the Bristol road, but during that summer a 'King' was used on the Saturday 'Bristolian' which on a slower schedule ran through to Weston-super-Mare. Engine and stock

Paddington-Birmingham line expresses with
Old Oak motive power:

(Opposite top)
On 21 March 1960, the up 'Cambrian Coast Express' approaches Birmingham Snow Hill behind No 6013 King Henry III. *The engine would have worked down to Wolverhampton with the 8.30am ex-Paddington. By 1960, the up 'CCE' was the sole remaining Birmingham two-hour train.*

(Opposite lower)
Some of the '70xx' series of 'Castles' were highly regarded at Old Oak Common, and one of the favourites was No 7036 Taunton Castle, *seen storming past Ranelagh Bridge yard on 27 August 1960 with the 4.10pm Paddington-Birkenhead. This train was normally worked by a Stafford Road 'King' but for summer Saturdays such as this diagrams were often altered.*
Both: R. C. Riley

returned on the 2.35pm up. In the summer of 1963, Old Oak 'Castles' were used for this and one or two other Saturday workings to and from Bristol.

The 'Bristolian' apart, one of the hardest workings for an Old Oak 'Castle' during the 1950s was that covering the 'Cambrian Coast Express' through to Shrewsbury and back with the up train, a total of 306 miles within 6hr. Usually,

a specially picked engine was employed, one that was recently ex-works from Swindon and had been suitably run-in. The engine might stay on the diagram for several days - or more. For instance, No 7032 *Denbigh Castle* was used almost continuously between April and July 1957, and missed no more than five days during this period. A 'King' was the usual choice for this diagram after spring 1959 but then the timing of the up 'Cambrian Coast' was changed, and instead the engine off the down train returned from Shrewsbury with the 2.35pm Birkenhead-Paddington. Ted comments:

> The 'Cambrian Coast' turn was too much for one fireman to work throughout the week so the job was split: Monday, Tuesday, Wednesday in one part of the Link, and Thursday, Friday and Saturday in another part. The turn was worth a day's pay plus 21 hours' mileage. The 'Castle' was never coaled at Shrewsbury. Care was taken to fill the tender up well at Old Oak before setting out. We got off the engine, and went to a pub near the station for a plate of sandwiches, and a pint

Driver Walter Harris retired in 1957. Here he works on the 'Cornish Riviera' for the last time, leaving Paddington with No 6000 King George V
D. Matthews

or two. Meanwhile, the driver and a couple of fireman from the local shed who had relieved us brought the coal forward in the tender, and turned the engine on Abbey Foregate triangle. Once through Banbury with the up 'Cambrian Coast', you were reaching into the back of the tender for coal. When you were a fireman in the Top Link some of the drivers - by no means all - would let you have a go at the regulator, and on the Wolverhampton road usually we drove up trains south of Banbury. The driver did the firing.

As a result of the temporary withdrawal of the London Midland Region expresses via Coventry, the Paddington-Birmingham-Wolverhampton service was augmented as from November 1959. The 'Kings' remained in reasonable condition for a while. Nos 6009/10/2/6/21 - 'a sewing machine' - and 6026 were reckoned as Old Oak's best while Nos 6000/13/5/29 were 'hard to work with'.

The two-hour Birmingham-Paddington timings, with an intermediate stop at Leamington, were always considered to be hard work by crews, other than with the eight-coach load of a train such as the 'Cambrian Coast Express'. Writers on railways in the 1950s tended to be critical of contemporary performances on the Birmingham line, but talking of prewar days Driver Jim Street of 'Cheltenham Flyer' fame was recorded as saying: 'the hardest trains to keep time with...are the two-hour trains to Birmingham...' In the 1959/60 timetable, there were six out and back diagrams to Wolverhampton for Old Oak 'Kings' although the through working to Shrewsbury with the down 'Cambrian Coast' was later restored. The Birmingham line service went over to diesel haulage with the start of the winter 1962/3 timetable. Top Link steam working was nearing its end at Old Oak, and the last 'Castle' diagrams on the Worcester line expresses finished with the close of the summer 1963 timetable.

Servicing facilities for diesel locomotives were now available at Old Oak Common, and over the next couple of years work proceeded on demolition of the main steam shed and the construction of the diesel maintenance depot which was opened in October 1965. The remaining steam locomotives at Old Oak had been transferred to Southall in March 1965. By then, steam working on the Western Region was in its last months, and effectively ceased on New Year's Day 1966.

In a chapter that features Old Oak and Paddington, there could only be one setting for the final photograph! Old Oak's No 5040 Stokesay Castle *has arrived at Paddington with an up express and, with a pannier tank already attached for removal of the empty stock to Old Oak, the crew have placed the red tail-lamp on No 5040's bufferbeam and the 'Castle' will follow behind.*
C. R. L. Coles

10

'IN A HOTTER PLACE YE COULDNA BE'

Polmadie MPD

One of the most famous names among the ranks of major steam depots was Polmadie, Glasgow, renowned for its duties on West Coast Anglo-Scottish services but equally important for providing power for suburban passenger and heavy freight services. 'Polmadie shed was above all a close-knit community of railwaymen, and once boasted its own pipe-band, and enginemen poets...

In a hotter place ye couldna be is the second line of a poem written by Polmadie driver, Donald McLaughlan, and one of many poems from the steam age featured in *Steam Lines*, a book of railway poetry collected by Willie McLagan. Polmadie was described as 'hot' on this occasion, in the wake of the arrival of a shedmaster filled with reforming zeal. That was typical. Polmadie is well-remembered as the sort of place that forged reputations, whether they were enginemen, shedmasters, supervisors, union representatives, or indeed locomotives.

A former leading light in the Associated Society of Locomotive Engineers and Firemen referred to the shed as the University of Learning for Footplate Staff. Along with many

Surely one of the most attractive photographs ever of a Polmadie engine - No 46230 Duchess of Buccleuch *makes short work of Beattock bank in September 1955 as it passes Harthope with the Glasgow Central portion of the summer 10.10am from Euston.*

W. J. Verden Anderson/
Rail Archive Stephenson

Polmadie shed yard in the 1950s:

Motherwell shed's LMS '5' No 45176 stands alongside the home shed's 'Royal Scot' No 46121 Highland Light Infantry on 21 May 1958. No 45176's blue-backed numberplate glows noticeably!

The ash-disposal plant dominates the scene and overshadows Caley McIntosh 0-6-0T No 56154, one of Polmadie's allocation that 'also served'.

Both: F. W. Shuttleworth

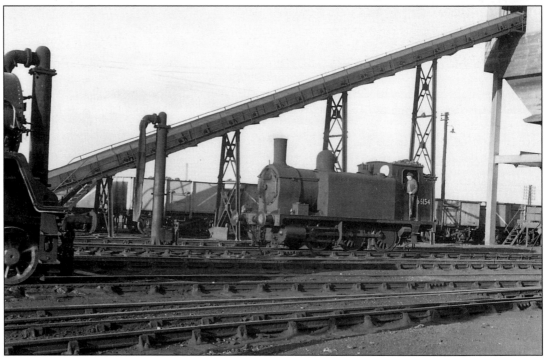

others, he never forgot his days at Polmadie. The place meant many things to those inside, and outside the railway. Its location was - and remains - on the up side of the main line to Motherwell and the South, 1¹/₂mile or so south of Glasgow Central.

Unlike many other such establishments, Polmadie is still working for the modern railway. It is West Coast Train Operating Company's base in Glasgow. In place of locomotives, these days its allocation comprises rakes of Mark 3 coaches used for West Coast's Anglo-Scottish trains, and

those of Mark 2s used by CrossCountry TOC.

'Pol-mad-ie'...a name associated with 'Duchess', 'Britannia' and 'Clan' Pacifics, 'Royal Scot' 4-6-0s, and not the least, 2-6-4Ts, all usually turned-out immaculately, many with pale-blue painted backgrounds to their smokebox number-plates.

The name has intrigued many people. As editor of *Steam Lines* Willie McLagan was no dilettante, but had served his time at Polmadie as fireman, fitter, driver, diesel driving instructor and headquarters' traction inspector. Yet he found

A fine study of Polmadie's 'Duchess' No 46221 Queen Elizabeth *waiting to depart from its shed for Glasgow Central in order to work the up 'Royal Scot' of 28 June 1954. At the time, a Polmadie 'Duchess' worked through to Euston with the summer weekday 'Royal Scot'. The enginemen are Driver Bob McLagan (William McLagan's father) and Fireman Joe Hunt of Polmadie. When Bob McLagan retired the following year, ten firemen attended his retiral 'do': this was a particular compliment to be accorded by firemen to a senior driver.*
John P. Wilson/Rail Archive Stephenson

time to research the origins of his workplace's name, only to conclude that there was no way of knowing whether the word derived from the Latin 'Poma die' - apples of God - on account of its orchards - or the Gaelic, 'Polmaddy', the haunt of the mad dogs or wolves among the marshes.

The name was well-established because from at least the 13th century there was a hospital for the needy, on a site near to that of the eventual locomotive depot. Then, during the 17th century, some local inhabitants were rounded up and shot for their religious beliefs. They entered the history books as the Polmadie Martyrs of 1685.

The fruit orchards, along with the pleasant Polmadie Burn, became a distant memory once the area had suffered the ravages of the Industrial Revolution. They were supplanted by coalmines, brickworks, a chemical plant, and waste-tips for the nearby iron foundries, all accompanied by engineering works. Of these, best-known in the railway world was Henry Dübs' Glasgow Locomotive Works. These workshops had been established at Polmadie in 1863, and were amalgamated with others in 1903 to form the North British Locomotive Co. Afterwards, the Dübs factory was redesignated Queen's Park Works.

The locomotive depot at Polmadie dated from the mid-1870s, and its origins derived from the Caledonian Railway's decision to build a line across the River Clyde from the south bank in order to serve a new passenger terminus fronting Gordon Street in central Glasgow. In 1873, the Royal Assent was granted to an Act which gave powers for the provision

of the new station, a locomotive servicing-point at Eglinton Street, and the running sheds and various sidings in the Polmadie area. Previously, the CR's principal shed on the south bank of the Clyde had been near the former South Side passenger terminus.

The new depot at Polmadie became the most important running shed on the CR, and from 1886-91 its Locomotive Foreman was one John Farquharson McIntosh. He had commenced his railway career as an engine cleaner, and then made his way up the ladder as a fireman, driver, inspector, and locomotive foreman, eventually becoming Locomotive, Carriage and Wagon Superintendent of the CR in 1895, a post he occupied until 1914.

Despite its importance, Polmadie's 1870s' locomotive depot was by no means an imposing structure, and the CR persevered with its timber buildings until the end of the Company's existence. In the first year or so of the fledgling LMS, a 14-road brick-built shed took their place, with sta-

(Opposite top)
By the mid-1950s, Polmadie men generally worked south of Carlisle only on the Manchester lodging turns, but the shed's Class '7' engines went through to Crewe. On 27 May 1956, the engine working a Sunday Manchester/Liverpool-Glasgow Central express is Polmadie No 70050 Firth of Clyde *whose crew are taking advantage of easy grades to let the 'Britannia' gallop through the Lune Gorge south of Tebay, and so build up speed for the climb to Shap.*
W. J. Verden Anderson/Rail Archive Stephenson

(Opposite lower)
Despite its allocation of 'Britannias', Polmadie persevered with the 'Clan' Pacifics and they continued to work some Manchester/Liverpool-Glasgow expresses. On 15 August 1959, the 4.15pm from Manchester Exchange gets away from Preston behind 'Clan' No 72003 Clan Fraser.
D. T. Greenwood/Rail Archive Stephenson

(Right)
Introduced in the summer of 1958, the second pair of 'Caledonian' expresses between Euston and Glasgow Central were worked by Polmadie 'Duchesses', No 46223 Princess Alice *of which is seen tackling the climb to Shap from the north.*
W. J. Verden Anderson/Rail Archive Stephenson

bling for 70 or so locomotives, and accompanied by a repair shop, and a mechanical coaling-plant. The reconstructed depot was completed by 1924/5, the repair shop having two 35-ton capacity overhead cranes, hydraulic presses and, in later days at least, a wheel-lathe. Notably, a wheel-drop was absent and, in BR days, some of the larger engines travelled to Eastfield to use the facilities there.

Though a 70ft turntable had been installed at Polmadie during the mid-1930s, along with a Kelbus sand-drying furnace, no major changes ensued until well into World War 2. Heavy wartime traffic to and from the Clydeside ports had considerably strained the city's railway facilities, and in 1941 the LMS decided to proceed with a modernisation scheme for Polmadie. This featured major alterations to the shed track layout, taking in land previously occupied by freight yards.

As rebuilt, the depot featured a reinforced concrete coaling-plant, a mechanised ash-disposal plant and new watering facilities. Outside the main building, a paved area surrounded concrete-lined inspection pits, complete with interior lighting, which were provided for each of the 14 shed roads. The turntable pit was relocated to the east end of the depot, and equipped with a 70ft diameter Cowans vacuum-controlled table. As modernised, Polmadie was reckoned to be one of the most up-to-date motive power depots on the newly formed British Railways. Even so, such modern facilities were not faultless. Breakdowns were recorded with the

ash-disposal plant, and also the coaling-plant, the latter the subject of some memorable 'runaways' when one or other of the three hopper doors had jammed open, with coal cascading to the ground.

From the turntable, engines moved to the coaling-plant, then to the ash-pits (noting that some engines did not have rocker grates) where their fires were cleaned, and the smokeboxes were manually emptied of char. Then engines generally proceeded on shed for stabling. The four parallel ash-pits in the disposal area each had steel grids, above which the contents of the engine ashpans were emptied into concrete hoppers. Having been quenched in a water-filled trough, the ashes were removed by electrically-driven conveyor belts which discharged on to a cross-belt travelling upwards to a bunker. Once loaded, the bunker dispensed its contents into waiting wagons which each day formed a small train to the nearest tip.

While the pre-1939 layout at Polmadie was difficult to work, the modernised post-1945 shed is remembered by Robert Taylor, the shedmaster from 1962-66, as 'well-planned - as good a layout as was possible for a steam shed.' Late in 1962, the depot's repair shop was converted to a diesel maintenance depot, fuel storage tanks erected near the coaling plant, and part of the running shed partitioned-off for use by Polmadie's growing allocation of Type 1 diesel locomotives. The earliest arrivals were of the 'English Electric' design now known as Class 20, but later deliveries were

of the unreliable and unpopular Clayton Type 1s.

On May Day 1967, the depot's 12 remaining steam loco-motives were withdrawn, BR Standard and LMS '5' 4-6-0s, and 2-6-4Ts. Steam had also finished on the Scottish Region as a whole. The transition from a major steam shed to a diesel depot had taken six years or so, and involved much more than the replacement of one form of traction by others. With increasing dieselisation and electrification, Polmadie accord-ingly reduced its intake of engine-cleaners. Manpower and duties had diminished in equal parts, and the 'steam culture' of the past century passed into memory.

Polmadie was a big place. Its staff complement numbered 1,150 in March 1962, shortly before 60 or so drivers were transferred to Glasgow Central in readiness for inauguration of the South Clydeside electrification, and thereafter they came under the control of the Area Manager. Of the 1,150 staff at Polmadie, 800 were footplatemen, 120 were artisan grades - fitters mainly - and the remainder comprised shed staff, labourers, and ancillary and clerical workers. Under the control of the shedmaster was the enginemen's hostel at Gushetfaulds, run by the redoubtable matron, Mrs Russell.

Under LMS control, Polmadie was coded 27A in 1935 as the Main Depot of a district that drew together the former CR depot at Dalry Road, Edinburgh, the CR and Glasgow & South Western Railway depots in the Glasgow area, and ex-G&SWR sheds in south-west Scotland. Later, the for-mer G&SWR depots were grouped in a separate district under the control of Corkerhill shed.

Following Nationalisation, a separate Scottish Region motive power organisation was set up in 1949, As a conse-quence, Polmadie was recoded as 66A, as the main depot in a district that included the sheds at Motherwell, Hamilton, and Greenock Ladyburn. In time, following the transfer of Carlisle Kingmoor shed to the London Midland Region and abolition of the '68' district, the Polmadie group of sheds absorbed those at Carstairs and Beattock.

Polmadie's shedmaster reported to the District Motive Power Superintendent, and although in BR days the post was no more highly graded than MS1 (the most junior man-agement grade) this and the corresponding post at Camden

were the only ones at former LMS depots so distinguished. Reporting to the Shedmaster was the Mechanical Foreman; two Foremen working shifts; six senior Running Foremen also working shifts; six 'inside' and 'outside' Running Fore-men, all on shifts; six shed arrangers, on shifts, mostly recruited from drivers, and an ash-plant foreman. This organisation largely followed previous practice. From 1966, the post of Shedmaster was redesignated Depot Engineer, and he now reported directly to the Regional headquarters instead of to the divisional running and maintenance engi-neer and the district motive power superintendents, both these tiers of management being abolished.

As at many locomotive depots, but more so than most, Pol-madie enjoyed a strong community feeling, fostered by a sense that its locality was somewhat isolated from the sur-rounding city. In some families, all their menfolk were employed in the railway industry, either operating trains, or involved in building locomotives at NBL Queen's Park. Most of the enginemen, fitters and shed staff lived locally in private rented tenements, or in the Govanhill and Gorbals districts. Many drivers and their families had moved during the interwar years to council estates, or into rented houses on private estates, and their place in the tenements was taken by firemen and other shed workers.

As elsewhere, there were the distinct groups of workers within the depot: the drivers, firemen and cleaners; the shed labourers; the fitters, and the office staff. It was said that when the enginemen were at work they talked about drink-ing, and when drinking their conversations were dominated by engines. Camaraderie and community spirit were strengthened by men's nicknames, variously obvious, or obscure in which case they recalled particular incidents, inspired or unprintable. Some men took exception to them, but most revelled in them.

Enginemen and others also came together in a variety of organised leisure and educational activities. The most obvi-ous perhaps were at the British Railways Staff Association Club which was set up after Nationalisation. There had been the Polmadie Pipe Band which in prewar years had been financed by the men, with some assistance contributed by the LMS. The pipers had the proud task of leading Glas-gow's trades-unionists and their banners in the annual May Day procession. A splendid photograph was published some years ago in the *Scots Magazine* of members of the band in all their glory alongside 'Coronation' No 6222 *Queen Mary*. Before much longer, members of the band had exchanged their uniform highland jackets for battledress to play their part in the Polmadie Home Guard, and turned out at Gourock to greet American and Canadian servicemen who had disembarking from troopships. A shortage of pipers later brought the band's demise.

The Polmadie Golf Club boasted many fine players and staged monthly competitions, culminating in a annual out-ing to Gleneagles golf-course where they were accompanied by wives and families. Composed mainly of cleaners, the shed football team was in the Glasgow and District Rail-

Here is the 9.25am Crewe-Perth in June 1957, with 'Royal Scot' No 46102 Black Watch *making an energetic ascent of Beattock bank past Greskine signalbox. The engine is displaying the blue-painted front numberplate and shedplate favoured at the time by some Scottish depots. One of the Beattock bankers is pushing at the rear of the train.*
W. J. Verden Anderson/
Rail Archive Stephenson

waymen's League. A well-supported first-aid and ambulance class was held on Sunday afternoons, with lectures delivered by local doctors. Attendance was voluntary. There was a practical sense of self-interest, given the hazards to be encountered in everyday work on the footplate. Membership of the Polmadie Benefit Fund provided for hospital treatment in the days before the NHS.

The Polmadie Mutual Improvement Class met on Sunday mornings, attended by drivers who wished to further their knowledge, and by firemen about to sit their technical examination and seek promotion to driving. The MIC movement had its foundations in the early days of the ASLE&F in the 1890s when the union had purchased models of engines for the instruction of its members. In those days, most sets of men had their own engine and off-duty drivers frequently gave up their Sunday mornings to attend to their pride and joy. Such activity led to discussion groups and was further stimulated by various books and pamphlets on locomotives which had been written by enginemen.

A fierce pride, and a strongly-held belief in the craft status of footplatemen were driving forces behind the MIC movement. At depots, the class followed guidelines set out by the national federation of MICs, and these included the election of officials, the collection of entrance fees, and the issue of membership cards. The general principle was that at meetings proceedings should be confined to study of the locomotive, and of railway rules and regulations. At other times, visits were organised to locomotive works, or to railway equipment manufacturers.

Drivers passed on their hard-won skills to firemen aspiring to become drivers. The process of tutelage was assisted within the class by lectures. These were given by enginemen or inspectors, and the subjects usually included valve gears, injectors, boiler fittings, controlled firing, and the operation

of vacuum and air brakes. The level of attendance at a class was usually influenced by the interest - or lack of it - shown by the locomotive inspectors who conducted the technical examination of firemen. Prizes were often presented to the member of the class attaining the highest marks in the technical examination. The minutes of the Polmadie MIC meeting of April 1945 record that 'all the members of our class who went forward to pass as drivers did so, and a number passed with high honours'.

The intention was that a suitable room should be provided for meetings of the MIC. This was often the railway's contribution, and sometimes comprised a grounded coach body, although until Nationalisation motive power organisations tended to keep their distance from the MIC movement. At Polmadie, the MIC met in the local ambulance hall until a new BRSA hall became available in the late 1950s. The movement died with the passing of steam, largely because BR provided enginemen with classroom instruction in the new forms of traction.

Among the workforce at Polmadie, the reins of power were in the hands of the Local Departmental Committee, and the local trades-union branches, membership of which was virtually 100%. It has been said that card-carrying members of the Communist Party kept a firm control on organised labour. Polmadie bred tough and often uncompromising people. They needed to be tough to survive in their chosen profession, and their steadfast opinions were a reminder of the early years of the century, and a response to tyrannical shed superintendents and autocratic management methods alike.

Yet, whatever the political - or religious - allegiances of some at Polmadie, there was never any doubt of a keenness to give the best to the job. The last Shedmaster at the depot was Robert Taylor who recalls 'a marvellous rapport' with the secretaries of the LDC during his twice-weekly meetings with them. Ian Lamb, who succeeded him in 1966 in the new post of Depot Engineer, remembers Polmadie for 'the best men ever I worked with. Everyone knew their job. Their priority was always the job although they might play hell with you. With full dieselisation, single-manning was introduced and, in order to distribute work and earnings more fairly, the mileage and spare links were abolished, at a time when the staff at the depot was halved. The scheme worked itself, thanks to the co-operation of the LDC, and the men.'

As elsewhere, whatever the status of the Top Link, these turns represented just a percentage of Polmadie's work. The majority of the shed's allocation of nearly 200 engines comprised 2-6-4Ts for local passenger workings from Glasgow Central, ex-Caley 0-6-0s employed on the numerous trip workings on the south side of the city, and WD 2-8-0s and 2-10-0s diagrammed to work steel and coal trains, such as those between the Fife coalfields and Clydesmill power station. The day-long local freight turns were often considered more exacting than double home passenger workings over well-maintained principal routes. Skill and careful judgment were called for in the days when freight trains were made up of wagons bereft of continuous brakes, and sharp gradients and poor trackwork were frequently encountered on the spurs into local collieries.

Polmadie men's route-cards were usually extensive although many enginemen were content to work only on local turns. Of those that worked further afield, the majority had 'signed for the road' to Crewe, Manchester via Bolton and via Wigan North Western; Preston; Carlisle; north to Perth and Dundee; to Edinburgh; to all Ayrshire coastal stations, including, at one stage, Stranraer and Girvan; and over ex-LMS lines north of the Clyde via Glasgow Central Low Level, including Balloch Pier.

What about the Top Link work in the latter days of steam? The No 1 Link consisted of 16-20 sets of contract mileage men. Their week's work usually comprised two return trips to, say, Crewe or Manchester, and a Sunday working. These were the double-home jobs to Manchester Victoria, Crewe

On summer weekdays, the Liverpool and Manchester portions of the morning North West-Glasgow express continued as separate trains north of Preston. This is the 9.43am from Liverpool Exchange, at grips with Beattock bank in July 1959. It is headed by Polmadie's No 46121 Highland Light Infantry, City of Glasgow Regiment *which is doubtless emitting that hollow, rhythmic exhaust so characteristic of these engines when working hard. In April 1959, this engine had emerged from Crewe after a general overhaul.*
David A. Anderson

and Perth, and also what were regarded as 'short-haul' workings to Carlisle and back, and the Sunday out and back short-rest passenger turns to Perth.

Thanks to Willie McLagan's foresight in presenting many of his archives and records to the Scottish Record Office, a full set of passenger engine and men's workings for Polmadie has survived. The principal turns with Class '1' trains for 1957 are summarised in Table 1.

These workings took care of the regular duties for Polmadie's 'Duchess', 'Britannia' and 'Clan' Pacifics, as well as the 'Royal Scot' 4-6-0s. In addition, there were plenty of relief and special workings. Crewe and Manchester were the customary southern limits of working for the shed's Class '7' engines, and by the early 1950s the 'Duchesses' generally went no further south than Carlisle. The exception was the 'Royal Scot' during the currency of the summer timetable. Except on Sundays, in each direction the train was worked throughout by a Polmadie Pacific.

In the early 1950s, Polmadie men in the top mileage link had worked as far as Crewe where they lodged. Either they worked the up 'Midday Scot', to return from there with the next day's daytime Birmingham-Glasgow express, or else they went south with the 'West Coast TPO', and the next day took over a Camden Pacific working to Glasgow with the down 'Midday Scot'.

On the double-home turns to Manchester, to take 1957 as an example, Polmadie men set out on a Newton Heath 'Jubilee' working the 4.5pm from Glasgow, and returned with one of their own 'Britannias' at the head of the next morning's 9.30am from Manchester Victoria. On another turn, at Carlisle a set of Polmadie men took over a Patricroft 'Jubilee' diagrammed to the 11.20pm Manchester Exchange-Glasgow sleeping car train; this engine returned south with a stopping train to Carlisle in the hands of another set of the shed's men. By 1960, for most of the week the 4.12pm ex-Manchester, and the following day's 10.50am ex-Glasgow were worked by Newton Heath engines and men,

Steam haulage of the weekday North West-Glasgow expresses was nearing its end on 18 June 1961 when Newton Heath 'Britannia' No 70049 Solway Firth *was photographed on Beattock bank with a Glasgow-bound train.*
D. M. C. Hepburne-Scott/Rail Archive Stephenson

TABLE 1 **Extracts from Polmadie (66A) weekday engine and men's workings from 16 September 1957**	**TABLE 2** **A profile of Polmadie's 'Royal Scots' from 1940-62**

TABLE 1
Extracts from Polmadie (66A) weekday engine and men's workings from 16 September 1957

Engine workings	Enginemen
Turn 6/1	
66A Class '8' engine	
10am Glasgow Central-Euston, the 'Royal Scot,	66A 8 Turn*
to Carlisle	12A 34 Turn
3.36pm Carlisle-Clasgow Central, the down	MX
'Royal Scot'	66A MO

*Regurned with engine working the 2.10pm
Carlisle-Glasgow Central Class '2' train*

Turn 6/3
66A Class '8' engine
9.25pm glasgow Central-Euston, to Kingmoor — 12A 34 Turn
7.15am Carlisle-Glasgow Central, the 12.10am — 12A 27 Turn
ex-Euston

Turn 6/4
66A Class '8'engine
10.20pm Glasgow Central-Euston, to Kingmoor — 12A 37 Turn
6.30am Carlisle-Glasgow Central, the 11.40pm — 12A 19 Turn
ex-Euston

Turn 7
66A Class '8' engine
Prepare engine
10.25pm Glasgow Central-Euston, to Carlisle — 66A 8 or 30
No 12 S/B — Turns out and
3.32am Kingmoor-Glasgow Central, the 10pm — back
ex-Euston
men relieved Glasgow Central

Turn 13
66A Class '7' engine - 'Clan'
11am Glasgow Central-Manchester Victoria, — 26A men MX
engine to Newton Heath — 12A men MO
9.30am Manchester Victoria-Glasgow Central — 66A men MX
— 12A men MO

This diagram was worked by two engines, out one day, back from Manchester the next day

Turn 14
SX working shown only
66A Class '7' engine - 'Royal Scot'
'A' engine
8.13am Glasgow Central-Edinburgh Princes St — 66A men
1.35pm Edinburgh Princes St-Glasgow Central
LE to 66A, then
11.15pm Glasgow Central-Birmingham New St, — Crewe 144
to Crewe — Turn
'B' engine
9.25am Crewe-Perth, to Carlisle — LMR men
7.50pm Carlisle-Dumfries-Glasgow St Enoch — 12A 37 Turn to
LE to 66A — Dumfries,
— relieved by 66A
This diagram was worked by two engines, — 19 Turn off
alternating as above — 5.30pm ex-St
— Enoch

TABLE 2
A profile of Polmadie's 'Royal Scots' from 1940-62

46102 *Black Watch*
Built 11/9/27, rebuilt 13/10/49 Mileage at 31/12/50: 1,319,731
Recorded at Polmadie from 11/4/42, transferred to Corkerhill 19/10/62, condemned 29/12/62
General Overhauls etc at Crewe incl boiler change: Gen 2-4/53; Gen 8-11/55; Heavy Gen 9-11/59
No Works attention at St Rollox
Mileages: 1956, 55616; 1957, 53,915; 1958, 48,263; 1959, 40,310; 1960, 54,597; 1961, 42,694; 1962, 21,437
During 1958: Six days waiting Works; 23 days on Works; 78 days running repairs and exams; not required, 1 day. Total: 108, a fairly average total for this engine during the 1950s.

46104 *Scottish Borderer*
Built 11/9/27, rebuilt 20/4/46 Mileage at 31/12/50: 1,272,960
Recorded at Polmadie from 11/4/42, transferred to Corkerhill 19/10/62, condemned 29/12/62
General Overhauls etc at Crewe incl boiler change: Heavy Gen 5-8/51; Gen 12/54-1/55; Gen 12/57-2/58
Light Casual and unclassified repairs carried out at St Rollox
Mileages: 1956, 51,338; 1957, 50,706; 1958, 50,150; 1959, 52,515; 1960, 58477; 1961, 42,649; 1962, 26,769
During 1958: 28 days waiting Works; 45 days on Works; 57 days running repairs and exams. Total: 130.
During the 1950s, the annual average of days waiting/on works, under repair or not req'd for this engine was 95-138.

46105 *Cameron Highlander*
Built 11/9/27, rebuilt 15/5/48 Mileage at 31/12/50: 1,322,597
Recorded at Polmadie from 13/2/43. Condemned at shed, 29/12/62, stored since 13/10/62
General Overhauls etc at Crewe incl boiler change: Gen 1-2/52; Gen 7-8/56; Gen 1-2/59; Gen (boiler not changed) 12/60-2/61
Mileages: 1956, 44,266; 1957, 50,172; 1958, 56,544; 1959, 53,180; 1960, 47,517; 1961, 45,203; 1962, 32,640
During 1958: Four days waiting Works; 15 days on Works; 76 days running repairs and exams; not required, 3 days. Total: 98. During the 1950s, the annual average of days waiting/on works, under repair or not req'd for this engine was 71-123.

46107 *Argyll and Sutherland Highlander*
Built 11/9/27, rebuilt 25/2/50 Mileage at 31/12/50: 1,239,949
Recorded at Polmadie from 11/4/42. Condemned at shed, 29/12/62, stored since 13/10/62
General Overhauls etc at Crewe incl boiler change: Gen 7-8/54; Gen 5-7/57 (Boiler not changed); Gen 3-5/60; Gen (boiler not changed) 12/60-2/61
Mileages: 1956, 56,452; 1957, 56,288; 1958, 57,035; 1959, 50,783; 1960, 52,624; 1961, 41,514; 1962, 36,184.
During 1958, the annual average of days waiting/on works, under repair or not req'd for this engine was 82.

46121 *Highland Light Infantry, City of Glasgow Regiment*
(named *H.L.I.* in LMS days)
Built 6/11/27, rebuilt 7/9/46 Mileage at 31/12/50: 1,489,720
Recorded at Polmadie from 23/7/49. Condemned at shed, 29/12/62, stored since 13/10/62
General Overhauls etc at Crewe incl boiler change: Gen 2-4/51; Gen 3-5/53; Gen 8-9/55; Gen 3-4/59
Mileages: 1956, 58,442; 1957, 52,932; 1958, 49,762; 1959, 45,644; 1960, 53,244; 1961, 43,211; 1962, 37,122
1958: Nine days waiting repair decision; five days waiting Works; 21 days on Works; 83 days running repairs and exams; not required, 1 day. Total: 119. During the 1950s, the annual average of days waiting/on works, under repair or not req'd for this engine was 69-127.

and the 4.30pm ex-Glasgow, and 9.30am ex-Manchester Victoria, by Polmadie.

Of those engines generally associated with Polmadie, 'Duchess' Pacifics were not on the shed's allocation until 1944 when brand-new Nos 6249-51 were taken on charge, to be joined the following year by Nos 6220-4/30-2/42 transferred from elsewhere. By the mid-1950s, the allocation of these fine engines included Nos 46220-4/7/30-2. Their duties were mainly on the heavy overnight sleeping car expresses, but one well-photographed working north of Carlisle was with the lightweight Glasgow portion of the summer weekday relief to the 'Royal Scot'.

Five 'Royal Scots' - Nos 46102/4/5/7/21 - were also closely associated with the postwar years of the depot. All but one had been on Polmadie's allocation in the early 1930s. Nos 46104/7 were regarded as the poorest of the five. In the late 1940s, and until the arrival of the new 'Clan' Pacifics, these engines were the first choice for the Manchester expresses. The 'Clans' arrived during 1952, and principally displaced 'Jubilee' 4-6-0s which had previously supplemented the 'Scots' on these trains. The five newcomers, Nos 72000-4, enjoyed a mixed reputation but one that was generally unfavourable. Willie McLagan says that their steaming was so poor that enginemen put 'jimmies' in the blastpipe to sharpen the blast.

During the late summer of 1954, Polmadie received 'Britannias' Nos 70050-4 fresh from Crewe Works. These replaced the 'Clans' and 'Scots' on the Manchester expresses, and generally proved superior. On a service notorious for poor timekeeping, the corresponding Newton Heath or Patricroft diagrams nevertheless remained in the hands of 'Jubilees' which were often sorely tried by 12 or 13-coach loads. Newton Heath finally received its own 'Britannias' early in 1960.

During the mid-1950s, a Polmadie Class 7' engine on the Crewe lodging turn worked through to Perth with the 9.25am train, stayed overnight in Perth, and returned to Carlisle with an Euston train. From this time, Aberdeen and Perth were frequently hosts to other members of the shed's Class '7' allocation which otherwise might be found on the summertime Glasgow-Liverpool/Manchester trains, or relegated to the Edinburgh stopping services. One engine was booked to work from Bell's Yard, Glasgow on the 5.55pm Dumfries-Kittybrewster fitted freight, to return south with the next day's 10.10pm Aberdeen Guild St-Dumfries. Polmadie men worked as far as Perth. Another '7' with a Polmadie crew was used for the evening 'Hie'lan Piper' named fitted freight which originated at Bells' Yard, and they brought back the next day's noon Perth-Polmadie Yard freight.

Twice, the first time in 1957/8, and again during 1960, Polmadie had temporarily bade adieu to its 'Clans'. Late in 1958, the depot lost two of its 'Britannias' for good when Nos 70053/4 were transferred to Holbeck. In time, the duties for the depot's Class '7' engines dwindled. Diesel locomotives which had arrived with overnight Anglo-Scottish freight ser-

vices were deployed on daytime services within Scotland, and dieselisation of the principal Manchester-Glasgow expresses was effected by the start of the summer 1962 timetable. By this time, none of the winter weekday Anglo-Scottish express trains was regularly diagrammed for steam haulage.

Combined with dieselisation of local freight workings, and electrification of the South Clydeside services, the shed's steam allocation was now left with the rump of secondary main line turns, station pilot duties, and diagrams on the Glasgow-Gourock suburban passenger turns. The last-named were largely steam worked until late April 1967.

By 1962/3, Polmadie's 'Duchesses', not to mention the Class '7s', were relegated to secondary and relief work which could be more economically handled by Class '5' power. And so, in common with other major Scottish Region depots, Polmadie began to place its surplus express passenger locomotives in store.

'Duchess' No 46227 went for storage at Lugton during 1962, and by the start of the winter 1962 Nos 46231/2 similarly languished at Carstairs. Polmadie also prepared to lay off most of its Class '7s'. At the shed, all five 'Clans', together with Nos 46105/7/21 of the 'Scots', and 'Duchess' No 46230 were to be found inactive, and devoid of their nameplates which were removed for safe-keeping. The two working 'Scots, Nos 46102/4, were transferred to Corkerhill to eke out their last couple of months' service. They, in company with most of the Class '7' and '8' engines allocated to Polmadie, were condemned during the final four-week period of 1962, and the first period of 1963. Survivors for a short while longer were 'Duchesses' Nos 46222-4/30/42/9 but, by the end of November 1963, Polmadie was without an LMS Pacific with the withdrawal of Nos 46230/49. In their place had come six LNER-design 'A2' Pacifics, Nos 60512/22/4/7/30/5 which, largely under-employed, lasted into 1965.

Robert Taylor comments on the decline of the main line steam power during his first couple of years at Polmadie:

The main line work was basically all-diesel by the end of 1963 although the shed was denied its own allocation of Type 4s to cover West Coast main line passenger duties, all of which were now diagrammed to be worked by locomotives based on the London Midland Region.

Primarily intended to cover the freight workings to and from Carlisle, the 'A2' Pacifics were never diagrammed to express passenger workings, although occasionally they deputised for a diesel failure.

Before we laid off the surplus main line steam power during 1962/3, engine availability had never been more than 66% - quite simply, too many engines were on hand. The old Caley 0-6-0s were well past their best. Their spindle-glands were worn, and it was impossible to keep engines like this steam-tight. We got rid of them as fast as we could. As withdrawals took place, the engine availability figures shot up. With fewer locomotives on the allocation, I was able to stop regular overtime working by fitters. No money was being spent on steam, and we had something of a hand-to-mouth existence in attempting to maintain their mechanical condition, and had to resort to cannibalisation. Having said that, by and large there were fewer failures with the steam locomotives than the diesels.

To my mind, there was no romance about steam. It was fine to watch the engines from the lineside, but when you were involved with their maintenance it was a different matter. It could be grim. The main challenge during my time at Polmadie effectively derived from operating two sheds - steam and diesel. It was not a good mix, and our diesel maintenance facilities were inadequate.

Matters eased somewhat when steam came to an end at Polmadie. The problem of disposing of locomotives was no longer there - now there was a big void in the middle of the shed, and the coaling and ash-disposal plants were redundant. The hostel was closed, and all the time the number of staff at the depot declined.

The first three months of 1963 were hellish. Locomotives in steam actually froze up, including their injectors, and the sieve-boxes in the water-tanks burst. To stop locomotives from freezing-up, we set up fires everywhere. Then when the thaw came, there were rows about the state of the place.

Polmadie's lack of adequate maintenance facilities for diesel traction contributed to its demise as a locomotive depot. During the late 1960s there were discussions within the Scottish Region as to whether just one diesel depot should serve all Glasgow. The choice went in favour of the former North British and LNER depot at Eastfield, despite Polmadie's location on the West Coast main line and its proximity to major traffic sources. In 1972, Polmadie's diesel locomotives, and their associated staff were transferred to Eastfield.

Today, Eastfield has been closed, and its site is a rubble-strewn wilderness. Polmadie survives, and retains remnants of its role as a steam depot, not least the looming repair shop with its massive water-tank that dominates Polmadie Road. Recent purpose-built facilities have been provided on site for the repair and maintenance of rolling stock, and Polmadie has gained a proud record for its modification and refurbishment of Mark 2 coaches. In place of 800 or so footplate staff, West Coast has just 27 drivers based at Polmadie for its duties. If realised, plans for new road construction would result in the demise of a place that boasts remarkable historical railway associations. Until then, Polmadie will retain some of its reputation for being 'hot'. And how did Donald McLaughan's poem conclude?

> Though hell we land in when we dee
> It'll no be waur than Polmadie

The translation loses something but may be interpreted as: Though we'll end up in hell when we die, it will be no worse than Polmadie.

The 'A2s' allocated to Polmadie after the withdrawal of the LMS Pacifics seldom rose above mundane duties, as typified by this Glasgow Central-Carlisle stopping train which, worked by grubby No 60535 Hornet's Beauty, *slows for the stop at Beattock station on 24 June 1964.*
T. G. Hepburn/Rail Archive Stephenson

11

RULE BRITANNIA

Pacifics working from Clacton

Not all the sheds with Top Link or express passenger working were household names. Take Clacton, for instance. This sub-shed to Colchester was responsible for some fine work with 'Britannias' from 1958-61. Much of what was done on the Great Eastern Line at the time gave some clue to what could have been achieved with steam in its latter days elsewhere on BR.

Clacton-on-Sea, $69^3/_4$ miles from Liverpool St station, was no more than a sleepy village when in 1867 the railway reached its coastal near neighbour of Walton-on-the-Naze. The junction with the main line was at Colchester. Clacton had to wait until 1882 and the opening of a single-line branch from Thorpe-le-Soken which became the divergence of the coastal branches. The line from Colchester was also single, and remained so until 1898. Over 40 years elapsed before the Thorpe-Clacton branch was doubled, and provided with full track-circuiting and semi-automatic colour-light signalling throughout. Until 1930, the Clacton and Walton lines had been subject to weight restrictions, and the 'Claud Hamilton' 4-4-0s were the largest engines allowed; in the 1920s, the loading of the principal up residential express had demanded the use of a pair of 'Clauds'. Thereafter, ex-GER 'B12s' took over.

Express passenger trains had worked between London and Clacton from the late 1890s, and by autumn 1910 there was sufficient residential traffic to and from London to justify building a set of corridor coaches - including a 'breakfast car' - to work the 7.3am from Clacton, and 5.6pm back at night. Local interests lobbied hard for additional services between Clacton and London, and featured in the major October 1914 recasting of GER main line services was a new fast train which reached Liverpool St in 95min (8min faster than before), and was balanced by a 5.30pm down to Clacton.

These trains continued after 1918. By the late 1930s, there were three residential trains each way, all with catering facilities. The fastest of these were counterparts of the crack trains introduced in 1914, and which now ran from and to Walton, not stopping between Thorpe and Liverpool St. The 4.57pm down from London was notable for its slip coach which lasted until 1939, and there was the Saturday midnight theatre train from Liverpool St-Clacton which in GER days had boasted a 'supper car'.

Such details give some clue to the importance of the residential trains between the Essex coast resorts and London. There were of course the holiday or 'buckets and spades' trains. Most of these were distinctly cheap and cheerful, but others were pukka expresses with restaurant cars. Much the

Britannia herself, waiting to leave Clacton-on-Sea with the inaugural up 'Essex Coast Express' of 9 June 1958. The distinctive headboard was soon dispensed with in favour of the more usual metal design.
G. R. Mortimer

same pattern continued after 1945, except that the success of Butlins' holiday-camp at Clacton boosted traffic on summer Saturdays. What was called the Clacton Interval Service was put on for the summer peak of 1950, when there were hourly trains both ways for much of the day. As with the other London expresses, at Thorpe these detached or attached their Walton portions.

Much of this pattern continued throughout the 1950s during which the Clacton Interval Service was an enduring feature of the summer timetables. Between Liverpool St and Clacton, the overall schedule of these trains was usually 2hr. Most of the through trains were formed of sets with buffet cars and were based at Clacton. The residential trains were generally hauled by 'B2' 4-6-0s allocated to Colchester, but sub-shedded at Clacton and worked by local crews. Clacton men's route knowledge was limited to the main line to Liverpool St, including the spur to/from St Botolph's Colchester, and, for purposes of working empty stock, the connections to Stratford Old Yard and Thornton Fields carriage sidings.

The 'B2's were Gresley three-cylinder 4-6-0s that had been rebuilt as two-cylinder engines. In time, they were displaced at Clacton by unmodified 'B17s', particularly Nos 61650/1/62/6. From the London end, Thompson 'B1' 4-6-0s working from Stratford shed were the usual choice for the Clacton trains as the 'Britannias' that had arrived on the GE lines from 1951 were concentrated on the Norwich service. In any case, the Pacifics were at this stage subject to a 40mph speed restriction between Colchester and Clacton. The timings of the Liverpool St-Clacton trains were unadventurous as compared to what was expected with the Norwich expresses.

During 1958, two developments combined to revolutionise

the Liverpool St-Clacton service, and to usher in an Indian Summer for steam. The previous year it had been decided to electrify the Colchester-Clacton/Walton lines at 25kV ac so that they could serve as one of BR's proving-grounds for high-voltage electrification. This resulted in Clacton having Britain's first public service worked by 25kV electric trains. In preparation for their introduction in 1959, the Great Eastern Line's management formed an Electric Link at Clacton to train drivers for the electric multiple-units assigned to the service. The senior passed firemen then at Clacton mostly opted to apply for driving vacancies at Stratford shed. Once there, they made an application for transfer to Clacton when a driver's job came up; nearly all made their return.

The other development released 'Britannias' to work the Clacton service. During 1958, the Eastern Region took delivery of ten 'English Electric' Type 4 2,000hp diesel locomotives. Five were allocated to Stratford depot, as an early stage in a scheme that aimed to displace steam entirely in the Great Eastern's London area. These five Type 4s were diagrammed to work Liverpool St-Norwich expresses alongside 'Britannias' but enough of these would be displaced to facilitate the acceleration of other principal GE Line services. Clacton crews were given some experience of the 'Britannias', immediately before they were introduced on the London expresses with the start of the summer 1958 timetable. By now, the civil engineer had lifted the restriction on their speed east of Colchester.

What was Clacton shed like in those days? It was located some $\frac{1}{2}$ mile outside the station, on the up side of the line, and had replaced the original shed which was on the south side of the station. The depot included a shed building with covered accommodation for four engines only, a turntable, a water column, and rudimentary facilities for coaling engines.

A morning Liverpool St-Clacton-on-Sea Interval Service gets into its stride past Gidea Park, east of Romford, behind Stratford 'Britannia' No 70041 Sir John Moore.
K. L. Cook/Rail Archive Stephenson

During 1958, work was in progress to adapt it from a purely steam depot to one that principally for the inspection and servicing of electric units.

The railway enthusiast's concept of a steam depot is usually of one with a mechanical coaling-plant, a vacuum or power-operated turntable, workshops, extensive stabling, and sets of men on 'prep' and disposal turns. The reality was that most steam sheds changed little from those known to Victorian enginemen, and relied on a measure of self-help from the crews. Shed labourers at such depots really laboured, and at Clacton, for instance, they were required to throw coal a distance of 8ft from wagons up on to locomotive tenders. The inset bunker of the 'Britannia's' tenders made their job even more difficult. Not long before steam finished at Clacton, a mechanical coal-grab was provided, and a shelter for the coalmen.

The enginemen at Clacton helped the coalmen who energetically warded off visiting Stratford men intent on topping-up the supply on their engines. For their part, a Clacton crew hoped to leave Liverpool St for Clacton with a full tender, having loaded up with a couple of tubs' worth of coal

at the station's engine siding.

Tom Wilson, a shed chargeman, was in command at Clacton shed, and Stan 'Dodger' Hall was his assistant. In charge of the stationary boiler for pre-heating the sets of coaches on the London service was 'Lumbo' Robinson. 'Nobby' Clark was the fire-lighter, and there were three coalmen. The enginemen's complement was 12 drivers, allowing for a man on rest days, 12 fireman (including five Passed men) and six Passed Cleaners. Fred Barral, Cliff Cockaday and Dennis Webb all worked from Clacton shed as passed firemen, and subsequently returned as drivers. Their reminiscences provide the detail and atmosphere of this chapter.

The mechanically-operated turntable at Clacton shed was capable of turning a 'Britannia', but only if the engine was positioned in the dead centre of the table, and with an almost empty tender. If not, enginemen risked distorting the centre pin, and the spares had to be ordered from Germany. On summer Saturdays, train operations were also hampered by a shortage of watering facilities at Clacton, made worse by low-pressure mains; on such occasions, care was taken to warn the crews of incoming engines that water should be taken at Thorpe.

The London-bound commuter settling down at Clacton to breakfast in the buffet car was unlikely to appreciate what had been involved in preparing his train. When the three-cylinder 'B17s' had been regular motive power, the fireman oiling-round had clambered-up to 'do the underneath' - the middle cylinder - in the pitch-dark of an Essex winter morning with the wind blowing off the sea. The driver meanwhile attended to the fire.

The last engine in at night, usually off the 6.33pm down from Liverpool St, worked the first London train the morning. It was the fireman's job to dispose of his engine and with a 'Britannia' the task was made easier by the rocking-grate and self-cleaning smokeboxes of these engines. Sometimes though the hopper pin stuck, or the rocker bars were particularly stiff.

Four main line engines only were stabled at Clacton overnight after 1958. Previously, one of the main line engines had run light to Walton in the morning to work the up residential train which originated there. Before electrification, also on shed was the locomotive that worked a morning local train to Colchester, and this was the back-up for the main line engines. Possibly, there might be another engine awaiting repair on the pit-road, and the fitter's attention.

The first engine off Clacton shed was the station pilot, usually a 'J69' 'Buckjumper' in earlier days, and this placed two of the train sets in the platforms for pre-heating; the others had been steam-heated already by the stationary plant. If a fireman was unavailable for one of the London trains, the man off the shunter took his place, and in turn was replaced

The publicity for the inaugural up 'Essex Coast Express' of 9 June 1958 included this early morning photo-call at Clacton with the driver of No 70000 Britannia *and local beauties. To the left of the picture are a Gresley buffet car and a restaurant car - nowadays the Clacton trains make do with a refreshment trolley.*
G. R. Mortimer

(Below)
The Great Eastern Line was determined not to be palmed off with the 'Clans', No 72009 Clan Stewart *of which made its trial runs to Clacton in the early autumn of 1958. Here it is pulling away from Colchester with the 3pm up Clacton Interval Service on 13 September. The journey time from Clacton to Liverpool St was 113 minutes.*
K. L. Cook/Rail Archive Stephenson

The down 'Essex Coast Express' forges up to Ingrave Summit from Brentwood on the evening of 23 July 1959, worked by 'Britannia' No 70039 Sir Christopher Wren.
K. L. Cook/Rail Archive Stephenson

by one of the engine-cleaners. The only early morning arrival at Clacton was the down 3.20am newspaper train from Liverpool St which used Platform 1. This was a duty worked by a Stratford engine and men.

For the summer 1958 timetable, two 'Britannias' on Stratford's allocation now worked diagrams based on Clacton. The first duty operated Saturdays excepted and began with the 7.51am from Clacton, a new service named the 'Essex Coast Express'. This was notable both for its lack of a Walton portion, and for the non-stop 80min booking between Thorpe and Liverpool St. The engine then worked to Clacton with the 10.36am down, back with the 1.54pm from Clacton, and returned from London with the 5.40pm down. As compared with the former 5.36pm, and despite the inclusion of extra stops at Chelmsford and Witham, this service had been accelerated 5min to Clacton on a 90min schedule from Liverpool St.

The second of the Clacton 'Britannia' diagrams covered the 8.14am up, this being the fourth of the morning residential trains, then the 11.36am down and 2.56pm Clacton Interval Services, and regained Clacton with the 6.36pm down. Outside of the summer service, that was the last of the evening's through trains. The star of the down trains though was the 5.27pm 'Essex Coast Express' with its 56min non-stop run for the $51^3/_4$ miles to Colchester, and an 86min timing to Clacton, and that was the fastest in steam days. Even with its fast timings the eight-coach 'Essex Coast Express' was not seen by enginemen as a taxing job for a 'Britannia' -

'it was easy for them - they simply flew along'. In that first summer, the down 'Express' was part of a Stratford diagram, thereafter it was worked by Clacton men.

Great trouble was taken to publicise the debut of the up 'Essex Coast Express' on 9 June 1958. No 70000 *Britannia* was the chosen engine, and six cleaners from Stratford descended on Clacton shed to ensure that the engine was turned out immaculately, and as a fitting backdrop for the bathing beauties who paraded for the benefit of press photographers. Clacton enginemen say that No 70000 'looked brilliant and sparkled, but then it should have done seeing how much effort had gone into its cleaning! En route to Liverpool St photographers and train-spotters were everywhere!'

Britannia spent much of its time at Stratford working the 'Hook Continental' boat train to and from Parkeston Quay, but enjoyed a somewhat uncertain reputation with the Clacton crews. 'It could be an absolute pig when its tubes were leaking!' is one comment.

The pattern of trains in the 1958 summer timetable changed somewhat as the result of the radical reshaping of the Great Eastern Line's services in January 1959. There were now four Clacton diagrams for the Stratford Pacifics:

Duty No 1	6.20am Clacton-Liverpool St
	9.30am Liverpool St-Norwich, and
	the 1.45pm return
	6.33pm Liverpool St-Clacton
Duty No 2	6.58am Clacton-Liverpool St
	5.27pm Liverpool St-Clacton -
	'Essex Coast Express'
Duty No 3	7.51am Clacton-Liverpool St -
	'Essex Coast Express'
	5.40pm Liverpool St-Clacton
Duty No 4	10am Clacton-Liverpool St
	3.33pm Liverpool St-Clacton

On a Norwich diagram, the 'Britannia' off the down newspaper train returned with the 8.14am Clacton-Liverpool St while the engine that had headed the up 'Hook Continental' worked down to Clacton with the 12.33pm down and back with the 4.15pm. Another Pacific took the 9.33am Liverpool St-Clacton and 1pm return, then the 4.58pm down residential and an up parcels train from Colchester and, yet another, the 4.36pm down and 7.55pm from Clacton.

For the four 'Britannia' diagrams there were eight sets of

In the later days of steam on the Great Eastern, the 'Britannias' may not have been clean but their sound mechanical condition was what mattered, and that was not in doubt. By now allocated to Norwich, work-stained No 70030 William Wordsworth *drifts down the bank towards Colchester with the 10.33am Liverpool St-Clacton of 5 September 1959.*
K. L. Cook/Rail Archive Stephenson

men, and a relief day cover. At Clacton, sets of men booked on from 5am onwards. After arrival at Liverpool St with the up trains, the 'Britannias' on Duties Nos 2/3 were worked light engine to Stratford by the Clacton men or with empty stock to Stratford Old Yard. The basic workings with the 'Britannias' were all out and home in the 1958/9 period but, once some diesels had been introduced to the Clacton trains, there were instances where the engines were 'unbalanced', and the men returned to Clacton 'on the cushions'. On Duty No 1, by which a 'Britannia' was returned to Norwich for its shed day, the Clacton men cleaned the outgoing engine's fire at Liverpool St's servicing-point, took water, and pulled the coal forward in the tender, and were relieved by Norwich men. Another set of men took over the incoming 'Britannia' that had received attention at Norwich, and worked home to Clacton.

Such changes had been accompanied by the transfer of all Stratford's 'Britannias' to Norwich shed. Dick Hardy was District Motive Power Superintendent, Liverpool St at the time and comments:

> The transfer away of the 'Britannias' was the best thing that could have been done. It was Willy Thorpe's decision to transfer them - at the time he was the Line Traffic Manager (Great Eastern). With the arrival at Stratford of main line diesels in quantity we needed to concentrate our resources on them. We had been desperately short of shed staff for tube cleaning and boiler washing. At Norwich, Bill Harvey was the shedmaster, and had an army of artisans at his command. With their transfer, the condition of the 'Britannias' markedly improved.

All the Pacifics were now in a pool, and though crews no longer had their own engines, all those working them were

proud of the class as a whole. The Norwich engines working Clacton's diagrams were whatever had been sent up to London. There was a tremendous spirit at Clacton with the 'Britannias'. By 1961, their last summer working GE expresses, the engines were never in better mechanical condition, even if grimy externally. Stratford, Clacton and Norwich men seemed determined that the 'Britannias' would go out in a blaze of glory - and they did!

Dick Hardy had been concerned that on those occasions when a 'Britannia' was unavailable to work the accelerated Clacton residential trains, punctuality would suffer. Clacton resident, Arnold Quick was a newspaper proprietor, and a self-appointed and most effective representative for the railway's interests in the Clacton area. 'If his train was late into Liverpool St, he was soon up in my office to find out why', says Dick Hardy. To demonstrate that time need not be lost should a 'B1' or 'B17' have to deputise on a Clacton train, Dick decided to prove the point himself. Before the introduction of the summer 1958 timetable, one evening he fired to Clacton Driver Stan Pittuck who was working the 5.36pm from Liverpool St with 'B17' No 61666 *Nottingham Forest*. 'Our aim was to get to Colchester as soon as possible, and I was able to show that one of the 4-6-0s could keep the Pacific timings'. Fred Barral comments: 'Most members of the class took a lot of handling, and No 61666 was by far the best of the 'B17s' at Clacton'.

Authorities elsewhere nurtured thoughts of transferring the smaller 'Clan' Pacifics to the GE Lines to cover the Clacton and other diagrams, and to redeploy the 'Britannias'. No 72009 *Clan Stewart* arrived at Stratford in September 1958 and spent just over a month on the Great Eastern 'on trial'. Dick Hardy recalls riding to Colchester on No 72009 when it worked the 5.40pm Clacton train. 'It did not steam freely, and its work was indistinguishable from a good "B1"'. Dennis Webb says he will never forget his firing turn on No 72009. 'I never put down the shovel. You had to fire continuously to keep time. By the end of the trip, the blade of my shovel was white-hot, and the shaft caught fire. The "Clan" was worse than a "B17", and Dick Hardy told us that he was determined to get rid of it.' He did, and the 'Britannias' remained on the GE Line until their displacement by 'English Electric' Type 3 diesel locomotives.

The 'Britannias' made the tightly-timed Clacton trains look an easy proposition, and perhaps the ignominious foray by the 'Clan' demonstrated the quality of the larger Pacifics when properly maintained and handled by men who cared about them - and timekeeping. When asked which of the

BRITISH RAILWAYS

Presented to
FREDERICK STEPHEN BARRAL
in recognition of

COURAGE AND RESOURCE

in going at personal risk to the aid of a colleague who had collapsed on the tender of an engine at Clacton-on-Sea after contact with the overhead live conductor wire on Saturday 22nd August 1959

H.C. Cohnson.

General Manager
Eastern Region

Fred Barral's well-deserved commendation, the circumstances surrounding which are described in the text.
Courtesy of F. S. Barral

Norwich-based 'Britannias' that worked the Clacton diagrams was the best, all three Clacton men had no hesitation in replying: 'There was not much in it - they were all the same.'

Cliff Cockaday commented: 'They were Rolls-Royces - other engines stood no comparison. There was always steam to spare. Ideally, they ran at 15-20% cut-off. Unlike the 'B17s', for instance, you didn't notice some of the sharp gradients on the Clacton line, such as the 1 in 110 climb to Alresford on the up line, or the climb out of Wivenhoe in the down direction. Another bad spot where the rails tended to be greasy in the morning was from Weeley up to Great Bentley'.

Fred Barral: 'I couldn't fault them for steaming or riding.

There was plenty of room in the cab as compared with a 'B1' or 'B17', and the cab doors on a 'Britannia' stayed shut which they didn't on a 'B17'!. On the 4-6-0s, the heat from the fire was blistering sometimes, but with a 'Britannia' you could open the roof ventilator. They weren't dirty to work in my experience - whatever has been said elsewhere. There was a sprinkler bar in the tender to keep down the coal-dust'.

Cliff Cockaday: 'If the tubes were leaky on a "Britannia", it wouldn't steam but only one in 1,000 was a rough trip. Normally, you could see the needle move up the boiler pressure gauge even when a couple of lumps of coal had been put on the fire. Fred Barral: 'You could count the number of bad trips on one hand'. On firing the 'Britannias', the three Clacton men's preferred method was to keep the back corners filled up. Fred Barral: 'I well remember my last trip with a "Britannia" on a Clacton train. It was on the Friday night before their final weekend on the GE. We had No 70009 *Alfred the Great*, and my fireman was a young chap from Colchester. Dick Hardy rode with us as far as Colchester. No 70009's tubes were beginning to leak, and you could see from the gauge that the pressure was hanging back'.

The exhaust injector on a 'Britannia' could be problematic. On one occasion, a crew working a down express from Liverpool St got as far as Romford, but were unable to get either the live steam or the exhaust injector to work. There was no option but to throw out the fire. Having done that, the 'Britannia' had just enough steam to shunt its train into the nearby sidings. A hard lesson was learned that big fires

shouldn't be built up at Liverpool St - or before starting from other stations, too.

Some of the wrinkles gained from working with the 'Britannias' on the Great Eastern derived from the need to avoid smoke, and blowing-off in Liverpool St station which was within the City of London's smokeless zone. In the station, and when awaiting release to the engine siding, 'You took care with the fire', says Colin Swettenham whose engine was No 70003 *John Bunyan* when he was a fireman at Stratford. 'The procedure was to turn the fire over left to right, then add coal to the bare bars. Then you turned over the fire on to the newly applied coal. You worked into the station with only half-a-glass of water, or less, in the gauge-glass. There was a dead section of overhead electrification at the platform buffer-stops ends so you could take water from the columns in safety'.

The Clacton drivers in the 'Britannia' link were younger in seniority to some of the firemen at other sheds, and that was a source of resentment. Fred Barral recounted an incident one day at the Liverpool St tea-hut. 'I was 32 and my fireman was aged 19. The Norwich drivers of the time were

Looking westwards, Clacton maintenance depot features on the left-hand side of this picture dating from June 1976, and the former steam shed is to the rear of the asbestos-clad stabling shed. A Class 47 arrives with a special train: like the Class 309 electric units in the middle distance the diesels and excursion trains are now as much a part of Great Eastern history as the 'Britannias'...
G. R. Mortimer

generally aged 50 or over, and the firemen in their forties. My fireman said to me, "Come on driver, make the tea!" You could have heard a pin drop. To the Norwich crews, I was too young to be a driver'.

Of the older Clacton drivers who mostly went into the Electric Link from 1959, Stan 'Chocolate' Pittuck is well-remembered as a good driver, and for his 6ft 6in height. Affectionately remembered was his habit of squatting beside his engine at Liverpool Street, pipe in mouth, and with his long legs sticking behind his ears up like a frog's. Passengers getting off the train were always intrigued.

Fred Barral was fireman when Bert Hudson made his last trip in service from Liverpool St to Clacton in 1958 or 1959. His regular 'B17' had been No 61651 *Derby County*. That run has stayed in Fred's memory, as he recounts:

'You take her down, Fred', said Bert, 'You choose the regulator and cut-off positions. I'll fire'. He got as far as Chelmsford which wasn't bad for a man on the eve of retirement.

In the early days of the Colchester-Clacton electrification, enginemen were faced with the ever-present hazard of the energised overhead wires. It had been second nature for a fireman to climb into the tender coal-space or to manoeuvre fire-irons indiscriminately. One August Saturday in 1959, Fred Barral saved the life of Stratford fireman Reggie Rowe who had worked to Clacton on a 'B17' at the head of an excursion train. When it came to the return working, the crew had intended to top-up the tender with coal. An argument had ensued with the coalman and, intention unsatisfied, Reggie went into the 'B17's' tender to find the coal hammer, and to pull coal forward.

Meanwhile, the 'B17' moved off shed and, once under the overhead, Reggie Rowe somehow touched the electrified wires. The shock threw him to the back of the tender where he lay partly draped over the backplate, with the rest of his body lying in water at the rear of the coal-space. Without a thought for his personal safety, Fred Barral hurried over to the 'B17', and climbed into the tender. While the driver summoned assistance, Fred extinguished Reggie's smouldering clothing, grabbed him by the seat of his overalls, laid him in the water to cool his burns, and held him in position until the 'B17' could be moved clear of the overhead wires. For his quick thinking and bravery, Fred was in due course deservedly presented with a cheque and framed certificate of commendation by the Eastern Region's General Manager of the time, Henry Johnson. Reggie Rowe survived his horrendous experience and has only recently retired as a driver at Stratford depot.

Such incidents served as a reminder that steam co-existed uneasily with the newer forms of traction. The Great Eastern Line had been chosen as one of the first sections of BR that would dispense with steam entirely. That happened finally in 1963. The 'Britannias' had ceased working to Clacton in 1961, and steam operations over the Colchester main line lasted only another year. By the autumn of 1962, Stratford shed had closed to steam. With 25kV electrification of the 'missing gap' between Chelmsford and Colchester, 1962 had seen the start of electrified services between Clacton, Walton and London. The next year, the AM9 'Clacton Electrics' had arrived, and soon won the admiration of railwaymen and their customers alike.

The adapted and extended steam shed continued in use for electric multiple-units until 1981. Its replacement was a larger depot with greatly improved facilities located adjacent to the station. The buildings of the abandoned depot were left largely intact, and subsequently partly incorporated into a car repair business. The 1981 depot fell victim to the privatisation process, and closed completely in March 1994 when all electric units based at Clacton were either withdrawn or transferred to Ilford.